the Bible
made Plain &
Simple

the Bible
made Plain &
Simple

MARK WATER

illustrations by KAREN DONNELLY

HENDRICKSON
PUBLISHERS

Contents

Part One: **Background to Bible Events** 5–27
6 Archaeology and the Bible 8 The Dead Sea Scrolls
10 Bible Lands 12 Bible Translations 14 Clothes,
Hairstyles, and Cosmetics 16 Travel 18 Homes
20 Empires of the Bible 22 Money 24 Music 26 Birds

Part Two: **Introducing Jesus** 28–53
30 A Chronology of the Life of Jesus 32 Jesus
Fulfills Old Testament Prophecies 34 Typology of
the Bible 36 The Birth and Childhood of Jesus
38 Jesus' Baptism and Temptations 40 Jesus'
Miracles 42 Jesus and Prayer 44 The Names of Jesus
46 Jesus' Last Week 48 Jesus' Death 50 Jesus'
Resurrection 52 Jesus Will Return

Part Three: **Introducing Bible People** 54–79
56 The Names for God 58 Old Testament People
60 Abraham 62 Moses 64 The Judges 66 The
Prophets 68 David and the Kings 70 The Twelve (1)
72 The Twelve (2) 74 The Pharisees, Jesus'
Opponents 76 Paul 78 New Testament People

Part Four: **Introducing Bible Teaching** 80–103
82 Teaching about God the Father 84 Teaching
about the Holy Spirit 86 The Parables of Jesus
88 Symbolic Language 90 Prayer 92 Humankind
94 What Jesus Taught 96 Salvation and the Cross
of Jesus 98 The Love of God 100 Satan Unmasked
102 The End of the World

Part Five: **Bible Summary** 104–127
106 How is the Bible Inspired? 108 Old Testament
Chronology 110 Setting of the Old Testament
Books 112 Pentateuch: Five Books of the Law
114 Historical Books of the Old Testament
116 Hebrew Poetry 118 Prophetic Books of the
Old Testament (1) 120 Prophetic Books of the Old
Testament (2) 122 New Testament Chronology
124 Setting of the New Testament Books
126 The Gospels' Teaching about Jesus

Part

1

Background to Bible Events

6–7
Archaeology and the Bible

8–9
The Dead Sea Scrolls

10–11
Bible Lands

12–13
Bible Translations

14–15
Clothes, Hairstyles, and Cosmetics

16–17
Travel

18–19
Homes

20–21
Empires of the Bible

22–23
Money

24–25
Music

26–27
Birds

Archaeology and the Bible

ARCHAEOLOGY

The word "archaeology," comes from the Greek *arkhaiologia*, meaning the science of ancient things.

The general field of archaeology embraces a study based on the

- excavation
- deciphering
- and critical evaluation of records of the ancient past.

Biblical archaeology

Biblical archaeology is a specialized branch of archaeology. It requires competence in both archaeological and biblical studies.

WHAT BIBLICAL ARCHAEOLOGY CAN AND CANNOT DO ʻ

Although archaeology is not meant to *prove* the truth of the Bible, it does demonstrate that the Christian faith is not based on myth, fairy tales, and magic, but on reliable historical facts.

THE EVIDENCE

Archaeological evidence which relates to the Bible record comprises:

- 25,000 sites, of which only about 200 have been excavated;

- Nearly 1,000,000 written documents, many of which have yet to be published.

Archaeological evidence comes in several forms.

PERIODS OF ANCIENT HISTORY

Archaeologists have traditionally arranged the earliest historical finds into three broad periods of time:

- the Stone Age
- the Bronze Age
- and the Iron Age.

When an artefact is unearthed it is assigned to a particular period of ancient history.

ARCHAEOLOGICAL PERIODS IN PALESTINE

THE STONE AGE

- Palaeolithic *(Old Stone)*
10,000–8000 B.C.—*Genesis 1–11*
- Mesolithic *(Middle Stone)* 8000–5500 B.C.
- Neolithic *(New Stone)* 5500–4000 B.C.

CHALCOLITHIC PERIOD

- Megalithic 4000–3500 B.C. (The Flood)
- Ghassulian 3500–3200 B.C.

BRONZE AGE

- Early Bronze 3200–2200 B.C.
- Middle Bronze
2200–1550 B.C. (Birth of Abraham)
- Late Bronze
1550–1200 B.C. – (The Exodus)

IRON AGE

- Iron Age I
1200–970 B.C. (David becomes king)
- Iron Age II
970–580 B.C. (Israel falls)
- Iron Age III
580–330 B.C. (The return of the Jews)

THE GREEK PERIOD

- 330–63 B.C.

THE ROMAN PERIOD

- 63 B.C.–A.D. 330 (Jesus is crucified)

"The progress of archaeological research will be found to constitute a steady march in the direction of establishing the essential trustworthiness of the Bible narrative, and greatly increasing our intelligent comprehension of it, and thereby our appreciation of its spiritual message, which constitutes its real value for mankind."

THE LATE SIR FREDERIC KENYON, FORMER DIRECTOR OF THE BRITISH MUSEUM

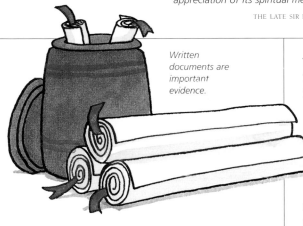

Written documents are important evidence.

ARCHAEOLOGICAL METHODS

The dig

A dig is the site of an archaeological exploration.

What to look out for

Clues about the age, history, and people of the site are gleaned from:

- Human remains
- Buildings
- Inscriptions
- Objects
- Written documents
- Weapons
- Coins
- Layers of ash (probably indicating fire).

DISCOVERIES

The Tower of Babel

Nearly 30 ancient temple-towers or ziggurats have been discovered in Mesopotamia; possibly one was the Tower of Babel, Genesis 11:1–9. One of the oldest dates from the fourth millennium B.C. at Uruk (biblical Erech, Genesis 10:10).

Tower of Babel

The Moabite Stone

The Moabite Stone, on black basalt, about 3 feet high and 2 feet wide, dating back to c. 830 B.C., was discovered in 1868 and commemorates the revolt of Mesha, king of Moab, against Israel (2 Kings 3:5–7).

The Cyrus Cylinder

The Cyrus Cylinder, discovered in the nineteenth century and dating from 536 B.C., tells how Cyrus captured Babylon without a battle and sent prisoners, including Jews from Babylon, back to their own lands, helping in the restoration of their temples. This is in line with Ezra 6:1–5.

INSCRIPTIONS

"Do not enter"

An inscription found in Jerusalem dating back to 30 A.D. has red letters on a white limestone block 2 feet 10 inches wide, stating:

"No stranger may enter within the balustrade round the Temple enclosure. Whoever is caught is alone responsible for his death which will follow."

This notice was placed prominently at the entrances to the Temple in the time of Jesus and his apostles and sheds light on the accusation the Jews made against Paul in Acts 21:28.

Pontius Pilate

An inscription with the name Pilatus (Pilate) was discovered on a stone from the theater at Caesarea in 1961, together with the name Tiberius, who was the Roman Emperor who appointed Pilate.

See also *The Dead Sea Scrolls*, pp. 8–9.

The Dead Sea Scrolls

DISCOVERY

If a young Bedouin shepherd had not lost one of his animals on the slopes of the Wadi Qumran at the northwest end of the Dead Sea in 1947, he would not have wandered into a cave where large jars containing leather scrolls had lain undetected for over 1800 years.

THE QUMRAN SETTLEMENT

The scrolls were the library of a religious group that had settled about eight miles south of Jericho over 100 years before Jesus' birth, as a splinter group of Judaism. The most important scrolls were found in 11 caves close to Wadi Qumran.

- Their settlement consisted of a *scriptorium* where the scrolls were copied.
- In their *potter's workshop* they made large jars that kept their manuscripts cool and safe.
- *A kitchen, bakery, storerooms, cisterns for baptisms and a cemetery* have also been excavated at the site of the Qumran community.
- Coins located there date its founding to about 135 B.C.
- The Jewish War of A.D. 66–73 forced this site to be abandoned and its precious manuscripts to be hidden safely in jars in surrounding caves.

The scrolls were discovered at Wadi Qumran, close to the Dead Sea.

THE DEAD SEA SCROLLS AND THE BIBLE

Out of the 500 substantial documents and fragments discovered, about 100 of them are books or parts of books of the Old Testament written in Hebrew.

The scrolls were copied in a scriptorium.

THE CAVES

Cave I

This was the cave where the first *accidental* discovery of the scrolls was made.

Cave II

Cave II contained nearly 100 fragments of Exodus, Leviticus, Numbers, Deuteronomy, Jeremiah, Job, Psalms, and Ruth.

Cave III

In cave III copper scrolls were found which purported to give directions to sites that contained treasure hidden at 64 locations

THE IMPORTANCE OF THE DEAD SEA SCROLLS

These documents are of great historical and scholarly value. Their discovery 1947–56 is most important in our understanding of the Old and New Testaments.

Archaeologists believe that the scrolls stored in jars in the first cave at Qumran were written or copied between the first century B.C. and the first half of the first century A.D.

The Dead Sea Scrolls show how accurate the previously known Hebrew texts are, but some scholarly theories about the late composition of certain Old Testament books are now no longer tenable.

The scroll of Isaiah.

throughout Israel. These sites have never been discovered.

Cave IV

Cave IV contained the most copies of Old Testament books found:
- Deuteronomy: 14 manuscripts
- Isaiah: 12 manuscripts
- Psalms: 10 manuscripts

These three books were the ones most frequently quoted in the New Testament.

Fragments from all the books of the Hebrew Old Testament except for Esther have been found.

A fragment of the book of Samuel, dating back to the third century B.C., was discovered.

THE SCROLL OF ISAIAH

The scroll of Isaiah (IQ Isa) was discovered in Cave I at Qumran in 1947. It is the oldest complete manuscript of a complete book of the Old Testament.

The scroll of Isaiah is almost 1000 years older than any Hebrew biblical manuscript previously known. Thus, the history of the Hebrew text of the Bible was pushed back by 1000 years at the discovery of the Dead Sea Scrolls.

See also: *Archaeology and the Bible*, pp. 6–7.

Bible Lands

THE PROMISED LAND

For Christians, Palestine is the Holy Land in the sense that it is a land distinct from all other lands. It is the Promised Land which Abraham was promised over 2000 years before Jesus' birth. It is the land where Jesus was born, lived, and died.

TWO RIVERS

The River Nile
Moses was put into the River Nile in a floating basket as a baby.

The River Euphrates
Abraham was called by God when he lived in Ur, just nine miles from the River Euphrates.

THE FERTILE CRESCENT

The events concerning the history of God's people, as recorded in the Old Testament and in the New Testament, can be said to have taken place between the River Nile and the River Euphrates. This area is often called the Fertile Crescent.

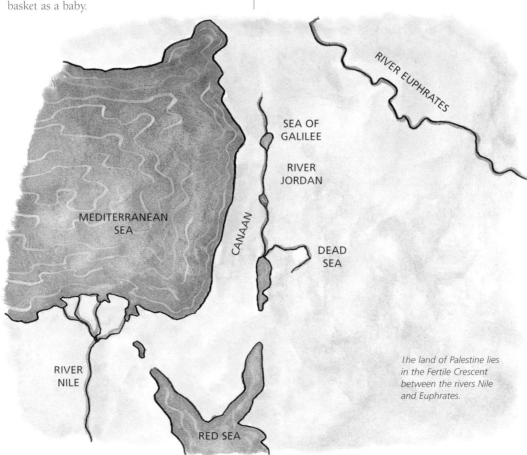

The land of Palestine lies in the Fertile Crescent between the rivers Nile and Euphrates.

THE LAND OF CANAAN

God promised Moses that he would bring the Israelites out of Egypt "into a good and spacious land, a land flowing with milk and honey" (Exodus 3:8).

Unfortunately Moses was unable to lead the Israelite people into this promised land—the land of Canaan—himself, as he died just within sight of it.

THE MAP OF PALESTINE

One way of appreciating the geography of Palestine is to split it into discrete regions.

The coastal strip
The name "Palestine" came from the territory where the Philistinians, Israel's enemies, lived, which was the southern part of this coastal strip, the Plain of Philistia.

The central highlands
In the north the central highlands start in Galilee, an area known to Jesus so well in his childhood and his public ministry.

The eastern tableland
The eastern tableland is a 250-mile-long plateau.

THE DEAD SEA

In the Old Testament the Dead Sea was called the Salt Sea (Genesis 14:3), Eastern Sea (Ezekiel 47:18), and the Sea of Arabath (Deuteronomy 4:49).

The Sea of Galilee was the scene of many of Jesus' miracles.

THE SEA OF GALILEE

The Sea of Galilee is called by four names by different authors in the Bible.
- The Sea of Chinnereth, or Chinneroth (Numbers 34:11).
- Lake Gennesaret. The Sea of Galilee is really a lake, and is called such (the Lake of Gennesaret [Luke 5:1]), by the much traveled Luke.
- Sea of Tiberias (John 6:1) appears to be the name some of the local people gave it.
- Sea of Galilee (Matthew 4:18) is the name we are most familiar with.

THE RIVER JORDAN

John the Baptist baptized people in the River Jordan. The river starts 230 feet above sea level and becomes 1290 feet below sea level by the time it reaches the Dead Sea.

See also: *Empires of the Bible*, pp. 20–21.

Bible Translations

THE FIRST TRANSLATION

The Bible was first translated in the third century B.C. in Egypt when the Hebrew Old Testament was translated into Greek.

JEROME AND THE VULGATE

Jerome, A.D. 345–420, was commissioned by Pope Damascus I to produce a scholarly text of the Latin Bible. He finished it in A.D. 400. It became known as the Vulgate version.

There have been many translations of the Bible over the centuries.

SOME TWENTIETH-CENTURY BIBLE TRANSLATIONS

Date	Version	Translator (s)	Description
1901	American Standard Version	Conservative scholars	Very literal translation
1952	Revised Standard Version	Ecumenical scholars	Revision of 1901 American Standard Version
1958	New Testament in Modern English	J. B. Phillips	Paraphrase in contemporary English
1976	Today's English Version (TEV)	American Bible Society	Uses simple, basic English
1978	New International Version (NIV)		
1982	New King James Version (NKJV)	Conservative scholars	Captures the ethos of the King James Version. Some scholars rate its translation of the Old Testament as one of the most accurate renderings of the Hebrew text.
1978, 1984	New International Version	Conservative scholars	Accurate contemporary translation
1990	New Revised Standard Edition	Interdenominational	Readable, dignified, with international experts' feel of King James Version
1995	Contemporary English Version	United Bible Societies	Aims to be read by the whole family, yet faithfully reliable.
1996	New Living Translation	Conservative scholars	Contemporary translation, not a paraphrase
1997	New International Version: Inclusive Language Edition	More than 100 scholars with New York Bible Society	Version of NIV using non-sexist language.

THE TRANSLATION OF PSALM 46:1

Coverdale (1535)	Geneva (1560)	Authorized Version (1611)
In our trouble and adversity, we have found that God is our refuge, our strength and help.	God is our hope and strength and help ready to be found.	God is our refuge and strength, a very present help in trouble.

WILLIAM TYNDALE
1484–1536

Because of opposition from English church authorities Tyndale was forced to leave England in order to translate the Scriptures. He published part of the New Testament in 1525 at Cologne and the rest of it in 1526 at Worms. In 1530 his translation of the Pentateuch (Genesis, Exodus, Leviticus, Numbers, and Deuteronomy) was published. On Henry VIII's orders he was arrested, tried, strangled, and burned at the stake.

Tyndale's translation of the Bible led to his death.

CHRONOLOGICAL TABLE OF SOME OF THE MAIN ENGLISH VERSIONS OF THE BIBLE

Date A.D.	Name of Bible	Translator	Description or Comments
Early versions			
7th century	English Verse	Caedmon	Versification of an English translation
	John's Gospel	Venerable Bede	He translated on his deathbed.
Middle English versions			
1380–83	Wycliffe Bible	John Wycliffe	With Nicholas of Hereford, Wycliffe translated the Bible into the speech of ordinary people.
Modern versions			
1525–6	New Testament	William Tyndale	
1530	Pentateuch	William Tyndale	
1531–4	Other parts of OT	William Tyndale	
1535	New Testament	Miles Coverdale	First complete Bible in English
1539–40	The Great Bible	Miles Coverdale	He incorporated the best of all English translations to date, including Tyndale's, but also used superior Greek and Hebrew manuscripts. This version became known as The Great Bible because it was prepared on huge pages, 9 in. x 15 in. (23cm x 38cm).
1560	The Geneva Bible	William Whittingham	The first Bible to be divided into chapters and verses. It was also called the "Breeches Bible" because of its translation of Genesis 3:7; "They sewed fig leaves together and made themselves breeches."
1611	The Authorized or King James Version (AV or KJV)	54 scholars drawn from Oxford and Cambridge Universities	Also known as "The King James Version Bible" because James I organized and supported it. For three centuries it was the most popular version in the English-speaking world.

Clothes, Hairstyles, and Cosmetics

CLOTHES

Many poor people only possessed the clothes on their backs.

The tunic

The tunic was a standard item of clothing. It was usually made of two strips of wool or linen sown together in the shape of a sack. A V-shaped opening was made at the top for the head, and holes were cut at the corners for the arms.

John the Baptist taught that: "The man with two tunics should share with him who has none" (Luke 3:11).

From John 19:23 we learn that Jesus' tunic or undergarment "was seamless, woven in one piece from top to bottom."

The cloak

This was another standard garment, but often only rich people could afford it. The cloak was worn on top of a tunic and a shepherd would snuggle into his cloak as he guarded his sheep in the open air through the night. If one were to offer a cloak as a pledge for a loan, it had to be returned to the owner at night so he or she could sleep in it (Exodus 22:26–27).

Footwear

Footwear consisted of sandals but many poor people walked barefoot.

HEADGEAR

Men wore headgear just as much as women.

Headcoverings for Israelite men

A square of cloth was folded into a triangle shape with the point falling down the man's neck and back. It was held in place with a circle of rope or cord that was wound round the forehead.

Turbans were also commonly worn by men, and rich Israelites' turbans displayed fringes.

Prayer shawls were worn to go to synagogue by all Jewish males from the age of 13. They covered the head and shoulders and had tassels dangling from each corner.

Phylacteries were tiny boxes containing Scripture verses, worn on the forehead and arm by men and fastened by leather straps.

Men and women both wore head coverings.

*Orthodox Jews still allow
their hair to grow long.*

Headcoverings for Israelite women

Women of Bible times wore veils which served
to protect them from the sun as much as the
men's headcoverings. But a woman without
a veil would also have been regarded as
immodest (Isaiah 47:2).

Hairstyles

The Jews, both men and women, let their hair
grow long. Orthodox Jews still observe the
custom of not cutting the hair at the sides of
their heads, and it dangles down in ringlets in
obedience to Leviticus 19:27.

ORNAMENTS

These were often considered to be
luxurious articles of dress.

Isaiah the prophet predicts that God's
judgment will fall on Jerusalem and Judah.

The "haughty" women of Zion "with
ornaments jingling on their ankles" (Isaiah
3:16) will not escape.

COSMETICS

Esther was given beauty treatments and
trained for six months in the use of
cosmetics and perfumes in preparation for
appearing before King Xerxes (Esther 2:12).

Xerxes was so taken with her appearance
that he eventually made Esther queen, and
she was later able to save the Jews from
being massacred.

Perfumed oils and ointments were needed
in the hot climate of Palestine to moisturize
the skin.

Eye makeup was popular. Ezekiel 23:40
makes a reference to eyes being "painted" and
Jeremiah 4:30 asks, "Why shade your eyes
with paint?" Eye makeup is sometimes
associated with prostitutes in the Bible.

Travel

A BOOK OF JOURNEYS

Today many people travel for pleasure. But not in Bible times. At best traveling was uncomfortable. Often it was dangerous. The travelers of the Old Testament were generally traders and soldiers. Other people traveled only occasionally to escape punishment or attack, to find food, to visit relatives, and especially to worship God.

Yet the Bible is a book of journeys. The story of the Jews begins with God's call to Abraham to set off on a journey. Jesus and Paul spent much of their time traveling, and Jesus' last command to his disciples was to travel to all parts of the world and teach everyone about himself (Matthew 28:19–20).

TRAVELING BY LAND

By donkey
Within Palestine, most traveling in both Old and New Testament times was done on foot. When the journey was tiring or there was luggage, everyone—rich and poor alike—went by donkey (ass).

By cart
Carts are rarely mentioned in the Bible because it was much easier to travel by donkey along the hilly rocky tracks of Palestine.

By camel
When the camel was domesticated around 2500 B.C. it changed the world. A camel can travel for three days without even drinking and it can carry baggage weighing up to 400 pounds.

By chariot
As well as war chariots there were traveling chariots, but they were used only by the wealthy and important, (Acts 8:26–28).

Travel by donkey or camel was more practical in Palestine than by cart or chariot.

Paul sailed to Rome in a grain ship.

TRAVELING BY SEA

The Egyptians

The Egyptians were skilled boat-builders. Their first boats were flimsy river craft made from papyrus reeds. Later they built strong wooden boats to carry huge building stones down the Nile from Upper Egypt. By 3000 B.C. they had mastered the craft of building sea-going boats.

Solomon's navy

Solomon was the only king of Israel to build a navy. But the Israelites knew nothing about boat-building and most of them had never seen a ship. So Solomon made a deal with the world's best sailors and boat-builders of his day—the Phoenicians. They built Solomon's ships, and then sailed them for him.

The Phoenicians were an ancient people who dominated sea trade during the first millennium B.C.. Much of their fleet was based at Tyre to the north of Israel. The King of Tyre also provided Solomon with materials to build the temple.

GRAIN SHIPS

Large grain ships regularly carried corn from Egypt to Italy. Paul sailed to Rome in two of these grain ships (his first ship was wrecked). Luke's detailed account of the terrible voyage reads like a ship's log. It is one of the best descriptions ever written of a sea journey in ancient times (Acts 27:1–44; 28:11–13).

Size

Length: 200 feet
Weight: Up to 1300 tons

Central mast

The central mast supported a square mainsail and a small topsail.

Front sail

This small sail at the front was used to help with steering. "Then they hoisted the foresail to the wind" (Acts 27:40). The grain ships were powered entirely by wind. Oars were only used in warships.

Steering

Two large oars in the stern steered the boat; there was no underwater rudder. In bad weather they were fastened in place with ropes so that the boat would hold its course in the waves and wind.

When Paul's boat came to land, Luke wrote, "they . . . untied the ropes that held the rudder" (Acts 27:40).

Homes

CAVES

The earliest homes in Palestine were caves. The limestone hills of Palestine are full of caves. They were rain-proof and kept people safe from wild animals.

TENTS

Tents were used as mobile homes by nomads, shepherds, and soldiers. The patriarchs all lived in tents. The apostle Paul earned his living by making tents.

Tents were used as mobile homes in Palestine.

HOUSES

The Israelites stopped living in tents and wandering around the desert when they settled in Palestine. Then their houses in the towns became very important to them. The word "house" appears more than 2,000 times in the Old Testament.

Houses were seen as gifts from God and when a new house was built there was a service of dedication (Deuteronomy 20:5).

When Jesus called heaven "my Father's house" (John 14:2), he was saying something immensely cheering to his mournful friends.

Types of houses

Many people lived in a small square box of a house. The whole family slept in one room, along with their animals.

Better houses had a wall outside enclosing a yard, which gave some privacy and space for the animals. People with more money added more rooms around the outside yard, turning it into a central courtyard. Really wealthy people added more and more rooms and courtyards and even had a second floor and basement.

CONSTRUCTION

Most of the poorer people lived in the simplest type of house.

The roof

These houses had a flat roof with a slight curve to allow the rain to run off into a gutter.

Stairs were on the outside of the wall instead of inside the house.

People went up on the roof to pray. Peter was using a roof of a house for this

Houses had an outside staircase leading to the roof.

purpose when he had his vision about clean and unclean animals: "About noon . . . Peter went up on the roof to pray" (Acts 10:9).

Parties were held on the roof, and during warm nights they often slept on the roof. Grapes and figs were spread out to dry. Rooftops in the Middle East are still used for drying grain or stalks.

Building a roof

To build a roof, beams of wood were laid across the top of the house. Branches were crisscrossed over and around these beams. Then the whole surface was covered with clay mixed with stones.

Because there were not many tall trees, the rooms or room was quite narrow—only about 6 foot 6 inches wide.

Walls

In rocky areas, walls were made from rubble and stones. Bricks were made out of straw and mud and then baked hard in ovens or in the sun.

When Jesus told his parable about the two houses, one built on a rock and the other built on sand, (Matthew 7:24–27), his hearers would have immediately understood. They all

Walls were made from rubble and stones.

It was important to build houses with firm foundations because of the risk of earthquakes.

knew that since Palestine was an area prone to earthquakes, foundations were crucial when building a house.

Inside the house

- Windows were small in order to keep the house cool in summer and warm in winter. Many simple houses contained just one window.
- Family area: the raised platform was made from stone or mud and stone chippings. People lived outdoors and on the roof as much as possible. There was no privacy. If people wanted to be alone, they went out into the hills and fields, as Jesus often did.
- Area for animals at night: the floor was compacted earth.
- Light came in through the open door, but the room was still gloomy and smelly. There were no chimneys, so the room became smoke-filled.

Upper room

More substantial houses had a first floor or upper room. Jesus and his apostles ate the Passover in an upper room like this (Luke 22:11–12).

Empires of the Bible

THE SEEDBED OF THE WORLD

The story of the Bible is acted out in what today we call the Middle East. It has been described as "the seedbed of the world" because many skills, such as farming, writing, and metalworking, were first developed in this area.

CANAAN

Canaan was an area that included parts of what is now Israel and Lebanon. It linked three continents—Europe, Asia, and Africa.

Much of the trade between these continents passed through Canaan and they all wanted to control it. They each succeeded at different times.

LEADING NATIONS

These are the most important nations of the ancient world from 4000 years before Jesus was born to the time of his birth.

Sumer

A notable non-Semitic culture appeared in South Mesopotamia (Sumer) over 5000 years before Christ. By 3000 B.C. Sumerian city-states like Kish, Lagash, and Ur developed considerable power, which was based on irrigated agriculture.

Egypt

The Egyptian civilization developed in the valley of the Nile over 5000 years ago. Moses grew up in a Pharaoh's court and benefitted from a high-class Egyptian education. It was most powerful from 3000–1000 B.C.

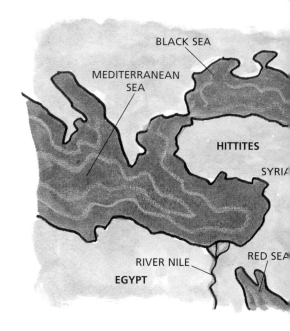

Hittites

They were based in what we now know as Turkey and were most powerful from 1600–1250 B.C.

Syria

From its capital city, Ebla, Syria was a wealthy superpower controlling all Canaan when Abraham traveled there. It was most powerful from 2400–1600 B.C.

Assyria

Today this is the northern part of modern Iraq. The prophet Nahum's theme was judgment on Nineveh, Assyria's capital. Its tyrannical cruelty scourged the ancient world from 850 B.C. to its fall in 612 B.C. Assyria destroyed the northern kingdom of Israel in 722 B.C.

Babylonia

Babylonia is also part of modern-day Iraq. Nebuchadnezzar II made Judah a vassal state in 605 B.C., but invaded when King Jehoiakim rebelled. A final invasion ended in Jerusalem's destruction in 586 B.C. Babylonia was most powerful from 612–539 B.C.

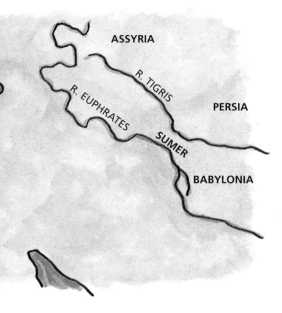

ASSYRIA

R. TIGRIS

R. EUPHRATES

PERSIA

SUMER

BABYLONIA

*Several nations dominated
Canaan during the development
of Jewish civilization.*

DURING BIBLE TIMES PALESTINE WAS INVADED AND ANNEXED BY FIVE EMPIRES:

The Assyrian empire

The Babylonian empire

The Persian empire

The Greek empire

The Roman empire

Greece

Greek success in the Persian Wars (500–449 B.C.) ushered in the golden age of Greek history. Alexander the Great spread Greek civilization and the Greek language across the known world. Greece was most powerful from 600–300 B.C.

Rome

The Romans conquered the world, and brought peace to warring nations. This prepared the way for the spread of the Christian faith. The Romans were most powerful from 275 B.C.–AD 210.

Persia

Persia is now northwest Iran. The Persian king Cyrus allowed the Jews to leave their exile in Babylon and return home. Persia was most powerful from 549–331 B.C.

TIME CHART OF EMPIRES IN BIBLE TIMES		
Dates	**Empire**	**Comment**
3000–1000 B.C.	Egyptians	Highly developed civilization
1600–1300 B.C.	Hittites	World power
1010–931 B.C.	Israelites	Golden age of King David and King Solomon
900–612 B.C.	Assyrians	World power
612–539 B.C.	Babylonians	World power
549–331 B.C.	Persians	World power
600–300 B.C.	Greeks	Golden age of Greek civilization
275 B.C.–A.D. 210	Romans	World power

Money

BEFORE CREDIT CARDS

People in Old Testament times did not have credit cards, and coins were not used in the beginning. At first goods were exchanged by bartering.

But very early on, in addition to bartering, people began to pay with bits of precious metal, such as gold and silver, or with silver jewelry or ornaments which were weighed out on scales (Deuteronomy 25:13–16).

CROESUS

About 600 B.C. Croesus, king of Lydia (today's Turkey), hit on the idea of making gold coins and stamping them with their weight. By New Testament times there were Roman, Greek, and Jewish coins, all of which had different values, and money-changers had a full-time job.

Goods were exchanged by barter.

NEW TESTAMENT COINS			
Name of coin	Metal	Equivalent to in coin	Comparison with another country's currency
Roman			
Quadrans	Bronze	4 quadrans = 1 as	
As (Gk: *assarion*)	Copper	4 as = 1 sestertius	
Sestertius	Bronze	4 sestertes = 1 denarius	
Denarius	Silver	25 denarii = 1 aureus	
Aureus	Gold		
Jewish			
Lepton	Copper		2 (Jewish) lepton = 1 (Roman) quadran
Greek			
Drachma	Silver		1 (Greek) drachma = 1 (Roman) denarius
Didrachma	Silver	1 didrachma = 2 drachma	
Tetradrachma (Stater)	Silver	1 tetradrachma = 2 didrachma	
Mina	Silver	1 mina = 2 tetradrachma	

"MONEY" IN THE OLD TESTAMENT

Wealth was reckoned by animals, silver, and gold.

Job, the richest man of his day, had 7,000 sheep, 3,000 pairs of oxen, and 500 donkeys (Job 1:3).

SHEKELS

In Canaan, silver was more common than gold, so gold became more precious. The Hebrew word for the basic unit of currency is "shekel" which comes from the verb "to weigh." Abraham weighed out 400 shekels of silver to buy a plot of land (Genesis 23:16).

Coinage was eventually developed and several different types were used in Palestine.

COINS

The first mention of a coin in the Bible comes in Nehemiah 7:71, about 445 B.C..

Coins and information

Coins were used to pass on information. When a new king was appointed, he minted coins with his head on them.

Roman coins

Roman coins are frequently referred to in the New Testament.

Jesus said that two sparrows were sold for an assarion, (Matthew 10:29).

The denarius is the coin mentioned most frequently in the Bible. Two denarii were paid to the innkeeper by the good Samaritan (Luke 10:35).

Jewish coins

The first Jewish coins were small bronze or copper coins minted between 135–104 B.C..

Only one Jewish coin is mentioned in the New Testament—the lepton, which means "thin." Its value was equivalent to one penny.

Greek coins

A drachma, made of silver, was equivalent to one Roman denarius. The drachma was probably the coin that caused all the trouble in Jesus' story in Luke 15:8–10.

BURIED TREASURE

In Palestine there were no safes, no drawers with locks, and no banks for ordinary people, so people often buried their money in the ground (Joshua 7:21; Matthew 25:25).

THE TALENT

The talent was not a coin, but a unit of monetary reckoning. Its value was always high, though it varied with the different metals involved.

The "ten thousand talents" in Matthew 18:24 is a figurative way of speaking about a very large sum of money.

Music

Bible writers took it for granted that everyone know what their music was like. Since they had no way of recording their music, we will never know exactly how their music sounded. But we can learn more about their music by studying the references to music in the Bible.

LOVERS OF MUSIC

People in Bible times loved making music. King Sennacherib of Assyria boasted in his court records that, as well as taking silver and gold from King Hezekiah in Jerusalem, he had taken Hezekiah's "male and female musicians."

Battle music and celebration music

Horns and trumpets carried messages in battle and called people to worship (Exodus 32:18; Numbers 10:1–7; Judges 7:18–20).

Whenever anyone felt happy, music was played. No one would dream of having a wedding or any party or celebration without music (2 Kings 11:14; Isaiah 5:12; Luke 15:25). Psalm 45 is a king's wedding song.

Sad songs

People also turned to music when they were upset. All the psalms in our book of Psalms were sung, not recited, and many were very sad, like Psalm 137:1.

David wrote a song when his best friend Jonathan died (2 Samuel 1:17).

Music was also played at funerals (Matthew 9:23).

Music while you work

Music has always accompanied work. In the Bible there are hints of the songs people sang:

- when digging wells (Numbers 21:17);
- when planting vines (Isaiah 16:10);
- when gathering grapes (Song of Songs 2:15);
- by a night-watchman on his rounds (Isaiah 21:11–12);
- as they marched (Numbers 10:35).

Music to worship God

People worshiped and praised God with music. The book of Psalms was their hymn book.

INSTRUMENTS

The instruments in the Bible can be divided into three categories: wind, string, and percussion.

Wind instruments

Pipe

The pipe (Hebrew: *halil*) comes from a word meaning "to pierce," and may have had a wailing, moaning sound. It was most frequently played at funerals, and in processions (Isaiah 30:29).

Flute

The flute (*masroqita*) comes from a word meaning "hiss" or "whistle," and it may not have been very tuneful.

Wind instruments may not have sounded pleasant to our ears.

Horn or cornet

The horn or cornet (*qeren*) was originally made out of an animal's horn but later out of wood or metal. This is one of the instruments that Joshua's priests blew when they attacked the city of Jericho.

Trumpet

There are different kinds of trumpets in the Bible. The shophar was also used by Joshua's priests and is still used in synagogues today.

The hasosera was also a priests' trumpet and was made of silver.

String Instruments

Lute

The lute (*shalishim*) was in the shape of a triangle and had three strings.

Lyre

The lyre (*kinnor*), translated "harp" in some Bibles, was an important instrument, played by priests in the temple and by the aristocracy.

Larger lyre

The larger lyre (*nevel*), sometimes translated "psaltery" or "harp," has the same name as "water bottle" in Hebrew. So the soundbox may have been round and fat, like a water bottle.

Percussion

Cymbals

There were two kinds of cymbals—the meziltaim and the silslim.

The meziltaim were "loud cymbals" and were two shallow plates, generally made of copper, which were clashed together.

The silslim or "high sounding cymbals" were hollow metal cups.

Sistrum

The sistrum (*menaanim*) worked on the same principle as a baby's rattle. It seems to have been made of small discs threaded on metal rods in a wooden frame.

Timbrel

The timbrel (*tof*), also translated "tambourine," was made from skin stretched over a hoop. It was held in one hand and banged with the other.

Birds

Palestine is a bird watcher's paradise. It has over 350 different species of bird. The Bible mentions fifty species and there are references to birds in 45 out of the 66 books of the Bible.

But in Bible times, people were not interested in bird-watching. There were eight types of owl, for example, but generally they were all called either "big owls" or "small owls."

King Solomon studied animals and birds and discovered that the natural world can teach us about God.

Migrating birds
Palestine lies below one section of a major air route for birds linking Europe and Asia and Africa. Each autumn and spring Palestine makes a handy stopping place for many thousands of birds.

Clean and unclean
The Old Testament divides birds into only two categories: birds which can be eaten ("clean" birds) and birds which cannot be eaten ("unclean" birds).

"Therefore I tell you, do not worry about your life, what you will eat or drink; or about your body, what you will wear. Is not life more important than food, and the body more important than clothes? Look at the birds of the air; they do not sow or reap or store away in barns, and yet your heavenly Father feeds them. Are you not much more valuable than they?"

Matthew 6:25–27

Birds which must not be eaten are the birds of prey (because they feed on flesh) and birds which eat fish.

Pigeons and doves
Pigeons and doves belong to the same bird family. They were "clean" birds that could be eaten and are the most important Bible birds because they were the only birds that could be offered in sacrifice.

When Noah sent out a dove from the ark to see if there was any land, he was doing what sailors used to do in ancient times when they were lost at sea. Noah's dove came back with an olive leaf, so for Christians the dove stands for hope and peace.

Most important of all, the dove represents the Holy Spirit. This was seen at Jesus' baptism: "As soon as Jesus was baptized, he went up out of the water. At that moment heaven was opened, and he saw the Spirit of God descending like a dove and lighting on him" (Matthew 3:16).

Eagles and vultures

Eagles are often mentioned in the Bible.

These were the hunters of the air—sometimes called "screamers."

The eagle's grace and power in the air are a source of considerable wonder (Proverbs 30:18).

Four species of vulture live in Palestine. The vulture often represents judgment (Luke 17:37). It was thought to be the king of the birds.

Raven

The Hebrew word for raven means any large black bird. Ravens live in lonely places and eat dead flesh (Isaiah 34:11; Proverbs 30:11).

They are unclean, hungry, greedy birds but God still cares for them (Psalm 147:9). Noah sent a raven out from the ark (Genesis 8:7), and ravens brought food to Elijah (1 Kings 17:4).

BIRDS IN THE BIBLE

Raven	Genesis 8:7
Dove	Genesis 8:8
Quail	Exodus 16:13
Eagle	Leviticus 1:13
Vulture	Leviticus 11:13
Red kite	Leviticus 11:14
Black kite	Leviticus 11:14
Horned owl	Leviticus 11:16
Gull	Leviticus 11:16
Hawk	Leviticus 11:16
Cormorant	Leviticus 11:17
Great owl	Leviticus 11:17
White owl	Leviticus 11:18
Desert owl	Leviticus 11:18
Osprey	Leviticus 11:18
Stork	Leviticus 11:19
Heron	Leviticus 11:19
Hoopoe	Leviticus 11:19
Pigeon	Leviticus 12:8
Falcon	Deuteronomy 14:13
Ostrich	Job 39:13
Sparrow	Psalm 84:3
Swallow	Psalm 84:3
Screech owl	Isaiah 34:11
Swift	Isaiah 38:14
Thrush	Isaiah 38:14
Partridge	Jeremiah 17:11
Hen	Matthew 23.37
Cock	Matthew 26:34

". . . those who hope in the Lord
will renew their strength.
They will soar on wings like eagles; they will run
and not grow weary,
they will walk and not be faint"
Isaiah 40:31

God cares for his children just as the eagle cares
for its young.
". . . like an eagle that stirs up its nest
and hovers over its young, that spreads its wings
to catch them and carries them on its pinions"
Deuteronomy 32:11

Sparrow

Robins, swifts, martins, finches, larks, blackbirds, warblers, cuckoos, and sparrows were common in Palestine and were all called sparrows or "twitterers." Children would catch them, kill them, pluck them, then fasten them together and sell them very cheaply for food. But even the utterly unimportant sparrow was important to God (Luke 12:6–7).

Roosters and hens

The main reason for keeping hens was not for food but so that there could be roosters to serve as alarm clocks in the mornings! "Cock crow" was another name for the time between midnight and 3 a.m. When Jesus said, in Matthew 26:34, that Peter would disown him "before the rooster crows" he was saying before 3 a.m. Jesus used the example of a mother hen caring for her chicks (Matthew 23:37) to illustrate his love for Jerusalem.

Ostrich

Today the ostrich lives mainly in Africa, but it could once be found right through Arabia and Palestine. In Job 39:13–18, there is a humorous description of the ostrich's stupidity.

Part

2

Introducing Jesus

30–31
A Chronology of the Life of Jesus

32–33
Jesus Fulfills Old Testament Prophecies

34–35
Typology of the Bible

36–37
The Birth and Childhood of Jesus

38–39
Jesus' Baptism and Temptations

40–41
Jesus' Miracles

42–43
Jesus and Prayer

44–45
The Names of Jesus

46–47
Jesus' Last Week

48–49
Jesus' Death

50–51
Jesus' Resurrection

52–53
Jesus Will Return

A Chronology of the Life of Jesus

DATE OF BIRTH

Why is Jesus' date of birth not given as 0 B.C. or A.D. 0?

Today many scholars believe that Jesus was born four, five, or six years before 0 B.C., in 4 B.C., 5 B.C., or 6 B.C.

One fixed point we have according to Josephus' *Antiquities of the Jews* is the death of Herod the Great occurring in 4 B.C. From Matthew 2:1 and Luke 1:5 we know that Herod was still alive when Jesus was born. So we conclude that Jesus' birth must have been no later than 4 B.C., and it could have been a little earlier, especially since Jesus was probably a toddler when the wise men visited him and Herod was still alive then.

Jesus' birth is now thought to have been in 4 B.C. or even earlier.

Dionysius Exiguus

The present Christian era was fixed by Abbot Dionysius Exiguus in the sixth century. Exiguus calculated that the beginning of the Christian era was 754 years from the founding of Rome. Abbot Exiguus did not decide the origin of the Christian era, he simply attempted to calculate it using what information he had. Today scholars believe that the Christian era should in fact have been calculated at A.U.C. (*ab urge condita*, "from the foundation of the city" of Rome) in 750 B.C. instead of 754. This fixes the date of the birth of Jesus as 4 B.C.

Jesus' ministry began when he was thirty.

EVENTS IN TH

Time	Event in the life of Jesus	Matthew
B.C.	**Introducing Jesus**	
5	Gabriel visits Mary	
5	Joseph's dream about Mary	1:18–25
	Birth and childhood of Jesus	
	Two genealogies: royal, natural	1:1–17
4	Jesus' birth at Bethlehem	1:18, 25
4	The angels and the shepherds	
4	Jesus circumcised and named	
4	The wise men visit Jesus	2:10–12
4	Joseph and family flee to Egypt	2:13–15
2	Joseph and family go to Nazareth	2:19–23
A.D.	**Eight years of silence**	
8	12-year-old Jesus visits temple	
	Eighteen years of silence/Year of inauguration	
26	John baptizes Jesus in the Jordan	3:13–17
26	Jesus is tempted in the desert	4:1–11
27	Jesus' first miracle at Cana	
27	Jesus expels temple traders	
27	Jesus meets Nicodemus at night	
27	Jesus meets the Samaritan woman	
27	Jesus heals a nobleman's son	
27	Jesus is rejected at Nazareth	
	Year of popularity	
28	Peter, Andrew, James, and John called	4:18–22
28	Jesus heals Peter's mother-in-law	8:14–17
28	Jesus' first Galilean preaching tour	4:23–25
28	Matthew follows Jesus	9:9–13
28	Jesus chooses his 12 disciples	10:1–42
28	The Sermon on the Mount	5:1–7:29
28	Jesus anointed by a sinful woman	
28	Jesus' second Galilean tour	
28	Jesus' parables about the kingdom	13:1–32
28	Jesus calms the Sea of Galilee	8:23–27
28	Jairus' daughter brought to life	9:18–26
28	The Twelve sent to preach and heal	9:35–11:
	The years of opposition	
29	John the Baptist beheaded	14:1–12
29	Jesus feeds 5,000 people	14:13–2
29	Jesus walks on water	14:22–2
29	Jesus feeds 4,000 people	15:32–39
29	Jesus asks the disciples who he is	16:13–20
29	Jesus is transfigured	17:1–13
29	Jesus at the Feast of Tabernacles	
29	Jesus heals a man born blind	
29	Jesus raises Lazarus	
30	Jesus blesses the children	19:13–1
30	Jesus heals blind Bartimaeus	20:29–3
30	Jesus meets Zacchaeus	
30	Jesus visits Mary and Martha	
30	Jesus' last week	
30	Jesus' resurrection appearances	

LIFE OF JESUS

Mark	Luke	John
	1:26–38	
	3:23–38	
	3:23–38	
	2:8–20	
	2.2:21	
		2:40–52
1:9–11	3:21–23	
2:12–13	4:1–13	
		2:1–12
		2:13–22
		3:1–21
		4:4–42
		4:46–54
	4:16–31	
1:16–22	5:1–11	
1:29–34	4:38–41	
1:35–39	4:42–44	
2:13–17	5:27–32	
3:13–19	6:12–19	
	6:20–49	
	7:35–50	
	8:1–3	
4:1–34	8:4–18	
4:35–41	8:22–25	
5:21–43	8:40–56	
6:6–13	9:1–6	
6:14–29	9:7–9	
6:30–44	9:10–17	6:1–14
6:45–52		6:16–21
8:1–9		
8:27–30	9:18–21	
9:2–13	9:28–36	
		7:11–52
		9:1–41
		11:1–44
10:13–16	18:15–17	
10:46–52	18:343	
	19:1–10	
		11:55–12:1

The Sermon on the Mount was central to Jesus' ministry.

Many of Jesus' disciples were drawn from the fishing community of Galilee.

Children were brought to Jesus so that he could pray for them.

See also: *New Testament Chronology*, pp. 122–123, *Jesus' Last Week*, pp. 46–47, *Jesus' Death*, pp. 48–49.

Jesus Fulfills Old Testament Prophecies

No chapter in the Bible tells us more about Jesus' death than Isaiah 53. The discussion begins at Isaiah 52:13.

PROPHECIES		
Predictions in Isaiah	**Theme**	**Fulfilled by Jesus**
He will be raised and lifted up and highly exalted. ⁊ Isaiah 52:13	Jesus' exaltation	Therefore God highly exalted him to the highest place ⁊ Philippians 2:9
He was despised and rejected by men. ⁊ Isaiah 53:3	Jesus was despised	The people stood watching, and the rulers sneered at him. ⁊ Luke 23:35
He took up our infirmities and carried our sorrows. ⁊ Isaiah 53:4	Jesus' work of healing	This was to fulfill what was spoken through the prophet Isaiah: "He took up our infirmities and carried our diseases." ⁊ Matthew 8:17
He was pierced for our transgressions. ⁊ Isaiah 53:5	Jesus was pierced	One of the soldiers pierced Jesus' side with a spear, bringing a sudden flow of blood and water. ⁊ John 19:34
The LORD has laid on him the iniquity of us all. ⁊ Isaiah 53:6	Jesus took our sin	He himself bore our sins in his body on the tree. ⁊ 1 Peter 2:24
He was oppressed and afflicted, yet he did not open his mouth; . . . he had done no violence, nor was any deceit in his mouth. ⁊ Isaiah 53:7, 9	Jesus' example of suffering	Christ suffered for you, leaving you an example, that you should follow in his steps." He committed no sin, and no deceit was found in his mouth." When they hurled their insults at him, he did not retaliate. ⁊ 1 Peter 2:21–23
He was assigned a grave with the wicked. ⁊ Isaiah 53:9	Jesus died with evil people	The robbers who were crucified with [Jesus] also heaped insults on him. ⁊ Matthew 27:44
He will see the light of life. ⁊ Isaiah 53:11	Jesus' resurrection	[Christ] was raised on the third day according to the Scriptures. ⁊ 1 Corinthians 15:4
He . . . was numbered with the transgressors. ⁊ Isaiah 53:12	Jesus himself claimed to fulfill this prophecy	"It is written: 'And he was numbered with the transgressors'; and I tell you that this must be fulfilled in me. Yes, what is written about me is reaching its fulfillment." ⁊ Luke 22:37
He bore the sins of many. ⁊ Isaiah 53:12	Jesus bore our sins	Christ was sacrificed once to take away the sins of many people. ⁊ Hebrews 9:28
He . . . made intercession for the transgressors. ⁊ Isaiah 53:12	Jesus prayed for those who nailed him to the cross	Jesus said, "Father, forgive them, for they do not know what they are doing." ⁊ Luke 23:34

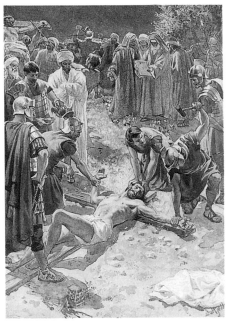

Jesus forgave those who nailed him to the cross.

Much of the Passion of Jesus was prophesied by Isaiah in the Old Testament.

Typology of the Bible

HOW "TYPES" ARE USED

In the Bible a "type" (from the Greek *typos*, "a blow or mark left by a blow; a pattern or impress") is a double representation in action. The literal represents the spiritual. So a type is the divine imprint of spiritual truth upon a literal event, person, or thing.

A study of the use of typology in relation to Jesus helps us to appreciate how Jesus fulfills Old Testament prophecies.

People as types: Cain and Abel

Cain is a type of the natural person, destitute of any adequate sense of sin (Genesis 4:3; 2 Peter 2:1–22; Jude 11).

Abel is a type of the spiritual person whose sacrifice of blood (Genesis 4:4; Hebrews 9:22) demonstrated his guilt of sin and his reliance upon a substitute.

Events as types

The Flood, the Exodus, the desert wanderings, the giving of manna, the bronze snake, and the conquest of Canaan are all examples of typical events. For example, compare Numbers 21:8–9 with John 3:14–15.

Cain was a natural type of person.

Institutions as types

In the many ceremonies commanded in the book of Leviticus, there is a concentration of typology.

Lambs and other animals slain to atone for sin (Leviticus 17:11) prefigured the Lamb of God (John 1:29; Hebrews 9:28; 1 Peter 1:19).

The Passover (Leviticus 23) portrayed Christ our Redeemer (1 Corinthians 5:6–8).

Actions as types

An example of a typical action is Jonah's experience with the great fish. It is a prophetic type of our Lord's burial and resurrection (Matthew 12:39).

Offices as types

Offices such as prophets, priests, and kings were regarded as typical offices.

For example, Moses as a prophet was typical of Christ in many obvious ways (Deuteronomy 18:15–18; John 6:14; 7:40).

Jesus was regarded as a great prophet by many who heard him, but few believed he could be the Messiah. It had been prophesied that the Messiah would come from Bethlehem, but Jesus was known to have come from Galilee (John 7:41–42).

Jesus' supposed ancestry, through Joseph, is traced in Luke 3.

Melchizedek was a priest and also displayed the office of a priest as a "type." "You are a priest for ever, in the order of Melchizedek" (Psalm 110:4).

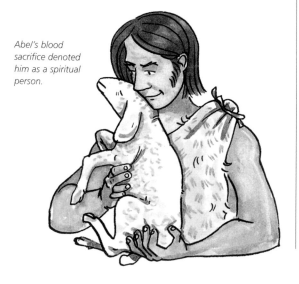

Abel's blood sacrifice denoted him as a spiritual person.

MESSIANIC PROPHECY IN THE BIBLE

Jesus is spoken about hundreds of years before he was born and in such exact terms that his appearing was clear to all who had spiritual eyes to observe.

MESSIANIC PROPHECIES

The Messiah would be:	Old Testament prophecy	Fulfilled In Jesus Christ
A descendant of Abraham	Genesis 17:7	Galatians 3:16
From David's family	2 Samuel 7:12–13	Acts 13:32
Preceded by a messenger	Malachi 3:1	Luke 1:17
Born of a virgin	Isaiah 7:14	Matthew 1:18
Born in Bethlehem	Micah 5:2	Matthew 2:1
The Shepherd	Isaiah 40:11	John 10:11–16
The Prophet	Deuteronomy 18:15	Acts 3:20–22
The Priest	Psalm 110:4	Hebrews 5:5–6
The King	Zechariah 9:9	John 18:33, 37
The Redeemer	Isaiah 59:20	Luke 2:1
Sold for 30 pieces of silver	Zechariah 11:12	Matthew 26:15
Mocked	Psalm 22:7–8	Matthew 27:39–44
Spat on	Isaiah 50:6	Mark 14:65
Crucified	Psalm 22:16	John 19:18
Resurrected	Psalm 16:10	Luke 24:6, 31, 34

Prophecies about Jesus left no doubt that he was the Messiah.

The Birth and Childhood of Jesus

No one knows what time of year Jesus was born.

Mark and John say nothing about Jesus' birth or childhood.

The first two chapters of Matthew's and Luke's gospels focus on the incarnation of Jesus.

The virgin birth

Mary was a virgin when Jesus was conceived in her womb. God brought this about in a miraculous way: "This is how the birth of Jesus Christ came about: His mother Mary was pledged to be married to Joseph, but before they came together, she was found to be with child through the Holy Spirit" (Matthew 1:18).

Jesus was born in humble circumstances, possibly in a stable that was attached to an inn.

Where was Jesus born?

Was Jesus born in a stable? This idea stems from the fact that Mary "placed [the newborn Jesus] in a manger" (Luke 2:7). Certainly, Luke informs us, "there was no room for them in the inn" (Luke 2:7).

Why December 25?

Nobody knows the month, let alone the day, when Jesus was born. December 25 was chosen to establish a Christian festival as an alternative to the pagan festival of the sun at the winter solstice.

Were there three wise men?

According to our Christmas cards, Melchior, Caspar, and Balthazar were the three kings who visited the infant Jesus. According to Matthew, these three visitors were following a star and are more likely to have been astrologers than kings.

Were Mary and Joseph poor?

Details gleaned from Luke's gospel indicate that:

- Mary and Joseph appear not to have been in a position to find suitable accommodation.
- Joseph offered a poor man's offering in the temple presentation—a pair of doves rather than a lamb (Luke 2:24).

THE EARLY DAYS

Caring for a newborn baby

Luke gives us a few details about how Mary cared for Jesus in the hours after he was born: "She wrapped him in cloths" (Luke 2:7).

Jewish mothers thought that a baby's limbs would grow straight if they were wrapped up firmly in bandages.

Circumcision

For a godly Jewish family, circumcision had a special religious significance. All Jewish baby boys were circumcised on the eighth day after their birth. It was an expression of faith dating back to Abraham's day, when God told Abraham, "You are to undergo circumcision, and it will be the sign of the covenant between me and you" (Genesis 17:11–12).

Naming

All Jewish babies were given names at a naming ceremony, often at the same time as circumcision: "On the eighth day, when it was time to circumcise him, he was named Jesus" (Luke 2:21).

The Magnificat and the Nunc dimittis

Two of the most famous Christian songs of praise are linked to Jesus' birth.

The *Magnificat* (after the first Latin word meaning to magnify) are Mary's words of praise, uttered when she visited her relative Elizabeth (Luke 1:46–55).

The *Nunc dimittis* (after the first Latin words meaning "now send away") are Simeon's words of praise as he took the eight-day-old baby Jesus in his arms (Luke 2:28–32).

Jesus' childhood would have been much the same as that of other Jewish children.

JESUS' CHILDHOOD

The only detail the New Testament gives us about Jesus' childhood is his visit to the temple in Jerusalem when he was 12 (Luke 2:41–52).

Escape to Egypt

Matthew records that Joseph responded to two more dreams and fled with Mary and Jesus to Egypt to escape the murderous intentions of King Herod and then, after Herod's death, "went and lived in a town called Nazareth" (Matthew 2:23).

Jesus' Baptism and Temptations

JESUS' BAPTISM

The Gospel record
"As soon as Jesus was baptized, he went up out of the water. At that moment heaven was opened, and he saw the Spirit of God descending like a dove and lighting on him. And a voice from heaven said, 'This is my Son, whom I love; with him I am well pleased'" (Matthew 3:16–17).

The Spirit of God
The Holy Spirit came on Jesus, not to overcome his sin (Jesus was without sin), but to equip him for his work. In Judges 3:10, "the Spirit of the LORD came upon [Othniel] so that he became Israel's judge." In the synagogue at Nazareth (Luke 4:18) Jesus claimed that he had been anointed.

The Holy Spirit descended on Jesus like a dove after John had baptized him.

> "No temptation has seized you except what is common to all people. And God is faithful; he will not let you be tempted beyond what you can bear. But when you are tempted, he will also provide a way out so that you can stand up under it."
>
> ↬ *1 Corinthians 10:13*

The dove
"…descending like a *dove*."
The dove symbolized gentleness, guilelessness, and purity (Matthew 10:16).

The Old Testament quotation
The words spoken by the "voice from heaven" are allusions to two Old Testament verses (Psalm 2:7 and Isaiah 42:1).

Since Jesus was sinless why was he baptised?
Jesus was "born under law" (Galatians 4:4), and, as Jesus informed John, "it is proper for us to do this to fulfill all righteousness" (Matthew 3:15).

"To fulfill all righteousness" meant the righteousness of obedience to the Mosaic law. The Levitical law said that all priests had to be consecrated as they started their work, usually when they were about 30 years old (Numbers 4:3).

Luke says, "Now Jesus himself was about thirty years old when he began his ministry" (3:23).

So for Jesus, the baptism signified the beginning of his ministry, although the legal requirement was not relevant in his particular case.

The Holy Spirit led Jesus into the desert to be tempted by Satan.

OLD TESTAMENT CONSECRATION

This consecration consisted of two parts, "wash them with water . . . take the anointing oil and anoint him by pouring it on his head (Exodus 29:4–7).

Jesus' baptism divinely consecrated him for his life's work—the work of redemption.

The purposes of Jesus' baptism

In addition to showing that God fully approved of Jesus, Jesus' baptism had certain other purposes. It:

- publicly declared that Jesus was God's Messiah (John 1:31–34)
- Jesus identified himself with our sin, for he had no sin of his own and became our substitute (2 Corinthians 5:21).
- Jesus left an example for his disciples to follow (Matthew 28:19–20). He instructed them to spread his word to all nations and to baptize them

JESUS' TEMPTATIONS

Jesus' temptations were not some kind of punishment because he had done something wrong. The Holy Spirit "led" him "into the desert to be tempted by the devil" (Matthew 4:1).

Jesus was tempted

The Greek word can also mean "tested." Either way this indicates the truth of Hebrews 2:18: "Because he himself suffered when he was tempted, he is able to help those who are being tempted."

"It is written"

In reply to each temptation Jesus said, "It is written." Then he went on to quote from a verse in the Old Testament (Deuteronomy 8:3; 6:16; 6:13).

LED BY THE SPIRIT	
The temptation	**The answer to the temptation**
"Tell these stones to become bread."	"Man shall not live by bread alone, but on every word that comes from the mouth of God."
"Throw yourself down [from the temple]."	"Do not put the Lord your God to the test."
"All this I will give you, if you will bow down and worship me."	"Worship the Lord your God, and serve him only."

These temptations are recorded in Matthew 4:1–10; Mark 1:12–13; and Luke 4:1–13.

Jesus' Miracles

Nicodemus realized that Jesus was special from the miracles he performed: "He came to Jesus at night and said, 'Rabbi, we know you are a teacher who has come from God. For no one could perform the miraculous signs you are doing if God were not with him'" (John 3:2).

Jesus' miracles were signs about who he was
When John the Baptist languished in prison he sent his disciples to Jesus to ask him, "Are you the one who was to come, or should we expect someone else?" (Matthew 11:3).

Jesus replied by pointing out that what he did demonstrated that he was the predicted Messiah. He told John's disciples, "Go back and report to John what you hear and see" (Matthew 11:4; Isaiah 61:1–2).

A MIRACLE OVER THE DEAD

"Jesus went to a town called Nain, and his disciples and a large crowd went along with him. As he approached the town gate, a dead person was being carried out—the only son of his mother, and she was a widow. And a large crowd from the town was with her. When the Lord saw her, his heart went out to her and he said, 'Don't cry.'

Then he went up and touched the coffin, and those carrying it stood still. He said, 'Young man, I say to you, get up!' The dead man sat up and began to talk, and Jesus gave him back to his mother."

Luke 7:11–15

Jesus performed miraculous healings:
- The blind receive sight
- The lame walk
- Those who have leprosy are cured
- The deaf hear
- The dead are raised.

John's gospels and signs
John does not talk about miracles like Matthew, Mark, and Luke, but uses the word "signs" for "miracles." John says, "Don't just marvel at the miracles. Fathom the significance of the signs" (John 4:54; Isaiah 35:1–2).

A MIRACLE OF HEALING

"A man with leprosy came to [Jesus] and begged him on his knees, 'If you are willing, you can make me clean.'

Filled with compassion, Jesus reached out his hand and touched the man. 'I am willing,' he said. 'Be clean!' Immediately the leprosy left him and he was cured."

Mark 1:40–42

Many of Jesus' miracles involve healing.

Jesus cured blindness on more than one occasion.

A MIRACLE OVER NATURE

"During the fourth watch of the night Jesus went out to [his disciples], walking on the lake."

Matthew 14:25

THE RECORDED MIRACLES OF JESUS

	Matthew	Mark	Luke	John
Miracles of healing				
Man with leprosy	8:2–4	1:40–42	5:12–13	
Roman centurion's servant	8:5–13		7:1–10	
Peter's mother-in-law	8:14–15	1:30–31	4:38–39	
Two men from Gadara	8:28–34	5:1–5	8:27–35	
Paralyzed man	9:2–7	2:3–12	5:18–25	
Woman suffering from bleeding	9:20–22	5:25–29	8:43–48	
Two blind men	9:27–31			
Man possessed and mute	9:32–33			
Man with shriveled hand	12:10–13	3:1–5	6:6–10	
Man blind, possessed, and mute	12:22		11:14	
Canaanite woman's daughter	15:21–28	7:24–30		
Demon-possessed boy	17:14–18	9:17–29	9:38–43	
Two blind men, one named	20:29–34	10:46–52	18:35–43	
Deaf mute		7:31–37		
Man possessed, in synagogue		1:23–26	4:33–35	
Blind man at Bethsaida		8:22–26		
Crippled woman			13:11–13	
Man with dropsy			14:1–4	
Ten men with leprosy			17:11–19	
The high priest's servant			22:50–51	
Official's son at Capernaum				4:46–54
Sick man at pool of Bethesda				5:1–9
Man born blind				9:1–7
Miracles over nature				
Water becomes wine				2:1–11
Calming the storm	8:23–27	4:37–41	8:22–25	
Walking on water	14:25	6:48–51		6:19–21
Feeding the 5,000	14:15–21	6:35–44	9:12–17	6:5–13
Feeding the 4,000	15:32–38	8:1–9		
Coin found in the fish's mouth	17:24–27			
Fig-tree withered	21:18–22	11:12–14, 20–25		
Catch of fish (1)			5:4–11	
Catch of fish (2)				21:1–11
Miracles over the dead				
Jairus' daughter	9:18–25	5:22–44	8:41–56	
Widow's son at Nain			7:11–15	
Lazarus			11:1–44	

Jesus and Prayer

Prayer was important to Jesus

- Jesus prayed after he performed a miracle: "After [Jesus] had dismissed [the crowd], he went up on a mountainside by himself to pray" (Matthew 14:23).
- Jesus prayed in solitary places: "Very early in the morning, while it was still dark, Jesus got up, left the house and went off to a solitary place, where he prayed" (Mark 1:35).
- Jesus spent whole nights in prayer: "One of those days Jesus went out to a mountainside to pray, and spent the night praying to God" (Luke 6:12).

Prayer is a way of communicating directly with God.

Two parables on prayer

The parable of the persistent widow (Luke 18:1–8)

"Then Jesus told his disciples a parable to show them that they should always pray and not give up. He said: 'In a certain town there was a judge who neither feared God nor cared about men. And there was a widow in that town who kept coming to him with the plea, "Grant me justice against my adversary."

'For some time he refused. But finally he said to himself, "Even though I don't fear God or care about men, yet because this widow keeps bothering me, I will see that she gets justice, so that she won't eventually wear me out with her coming!"

'And the Lord said, "Listen to what the unjust judge says. And will not God bring about justice for his chosen ones, who cry out to him day and night? Will he keep putting them off? I tell you, he will see that they get justice, and quickly. However, when the Son of Man comes, will he find faith on the earth?"'

The parable of the Pharisee and the tax collector (Luke 18.9–14)

"To some who were confident of their own righteousness and looked down on everybody else, Jesus told this parable: 'Two men went up to the temple to pray, one a Pharisee and the other a tax collector. The Pharisee stood up and prayed about himself, "God, I thank you that I am not like other men—robbers, evildoers, adulterers—or even like this tax collector. I fast twice a week and give a tenth of all I get."

'But the tax collector stood at a distance. He would not even look up to heaven, but beat his breast and said, "God, have mercy on me, a sinner."

'I tell you that this man, rather than the other, went home justified before God. For everyone who exalts himself will be humbled, and he who humbles himself will be exalted.'"

Jesus favored praying in secret.

JESUS' TEACHING ABOUT PRAYER

Jesus taught that we should not pray like the hypocrites: "And when you pray, do not be like the hypocrites, for they love to pray standing in the synagogues and on the street corners to be seen by men" (Matthew 6:5).

Instead, we should endeavor to pray in secret: "But when you pray, go into your room, close the door and pray to your Father, who is unseen" (Matthew 6:6).

The Lord's Prayer

The prayer we know as The Lord's Prayer from Matthew 6:9–13 and Luke 11:2–4, can also be called The Model Prayer or The Pattern Prayer, since Jesus originally told his disciples, "This, then, is how you should pray . . ." (Matthew 6:9). The context of the Lord's Prayer in Matthew shows that the Christian's relationship to God is not about outward shows of piety, but reflects the believer's love and devotedness to God.

Jesus' own prayers

One of the longest recorded prayers to be found in the Bible is Jesus' prayer recorded in John 17.

Its key idea is consecration.

The prayer breaks down into three sections:
- Jesus' consecration of himself (John 17:1–5)
- Jesus' prayer for his followers (John 17:6–19)
- Jesus' prayer for the whole church (John 17:20–26).

One of the shortest recorded prayers in the Bible is Jesus' prayer in the Garden of Gethsemane, just before he was betrayed by his disciple Judas Iscariot, arrested, and faced death by crucifixion, taking the sin of the world on himself: "My Father, if it is possible, may this cup be taken from me. Yet not as I will, but as you will" (Matthew 26:39).

Jesus prayed this three times: "He went away a second time and prayed." ". . . and prayed the third time" (Matthew 26:42,44).

JESUS' OWN PRAYERS

Jesus	Example	Bible reference
Whom Jesus prayed for		
Little children	"Little children . . . brought to Jesus for him . . . to pray for"	*Matthew 19:13*
His own followers	"I pray for [those whom you gave me]. I am not praying for the world."	*John 17:9*
His future believers	"I pray also for those who will believe in me."	*John 17:20*
God's glory	"Glorify your Son, that your Son may glorify you."	*John 17:1*
Those who killed him	"Father, forgive them, for they do not know what they are doing."	*Luke 23:34*
Himself	"Father into your hands I commit my spirit."	*Luke 23:46*
Simon	"But I have prayed for you, Simon."	*Luke 22:32*
Whom Jesus said we should pray for		
Persecutors	"Pray for those who persecute you."	*Matthew 5:44*
Demon-possessed	"This kind can come out only by prayer."	*Mark 9:29*
What we should pray about		
Temptation	"Watch and pray so that you will not fall into temptation."	*Matthew 26:41*

The Names of Jesus

BIBLE NAMES

Bible names were designed to tell you something about a person.

The names or titles given to Jesus do not tell us everything about Jesus, but they do tell us a great deal: that he was completely human and completely God.

THE SEVEN "I AMs"

These are seven names or titles Jesus gave to himself, recorded in John's gospel:

- I AM the bread of life (6:35)
- I AM the light of the world (8:12)
- I AM the gate (10:9)
- I AM the good shepherd (10:11)
- I AM the resurrection and the life (11:25)
- I AM the way and the truth and the life (14:6)
- I AM the true vine (15:1).

Jesus as "The Light of the World" in Holman Hunt's painting.

Jesus said: "I am the bread of life".

Jesus described himself as "the good shepherd" looking after his flock.

OTHER NAMES GIVEN TO JESUS

Name or title	Meaning	Bible reference
In the gospels		
Jesus	Jesus' first name, given by God. it means "God saves"	Matthew 1:21
Christ	Not a surname, but the Greek word for Messiah	Matthew 1:16
Lamb of God	Used by John the Baptist, meaning that Jesus was a sacrifice for sin.	John 1:29
Lord	In the four Gospels it was a respectful way of saying "Sir." Later it meant "God" and affirmed the deity of Jesus and his authority.	Luke 24:34
Master	A polite way of addressing someone, used by those who were followers of someone else.	Matthew 23:8
Rabbi	Similar to our reverend or pastor, given to someone who explained and taught the Bible	Mark 9:5
Shepherd	Jesus is the shepherd caring for God's people	Matthew 2:6
Son of David	Similar to "Messiah" but meaning that the leader will be a King, a descendant of King David	Mark 10:47
Son of Man	Title used by Jesus of himself, reflecting his human identity and his role as our representative before God	Luke 5:24
Son of God	Showing Jesus' unique relationship to the Father	John 20:31
Teacher	Similar to Rabbi	John 13:14
Word	A Greek title, *logos,* which John used to show that Jesus is the same as God and reveals God.	John 1:1
In the early Church		
Head of the body	A title showing Jesus' link to his church and to each of its members.	Colossians 1:18

Jesus also called himself a gate through which a person could pass to find pasture, i.e. salvation.

Jesus' Last Week

There are many details in the accounts of Jesus' last week which all point to the significance of his crucifixion.

Palm Sunday

The donkey was regarded as an animal of peace.

What happened:
Jesus rode in on a donkey: "They brought the colt to Jesus. He sat on it" (Mark 11:7).

Significant detail:
Since the donkey was a lowly animal, not a warhorse, and an animal of peace, Matthew was quick to see that Jesus riding into Jerusalem on a donkey fulfilled the prophecy from Zechariah 9:9.

"Say to the daughter of Zion,

'See, your king comes to you,

gentle and riding on a donkey,

on a colt, the foal of a donkey'."

⌒ Matthew 21:5

Monday: the fig tree

What happened:
"Seeing a fig tree by the road, [Jesus] went up to it but found nothing on it except leaves. Then he said to it, 'May you never bear fruit again!' Immediately the tree withered" (Matthew 21:19–20)

Jesus used the fig tree as a way of pointing out many Jews' lack of spirituality.

QUESTION:

Why did Jesus condemn the fig tree? "May you never bear fruit again."

ANSWER:

Jesus was acting out a parable. It was prophetic symbolism. The Jews would have known all about this. See Jeremiah 27:2, and 2 Chronicles 18:10 for this idea of an acted-out parable.

Significant detail:
The fig tree had nothing but leaves on it.

The leaves on a fig tree in Palestine appear in March, together with a crop of small edible knobs called *taksh* which drop off before the real figs form, which ripen in June. If there are no *taksh* there will be no figs. So just before Passover, in mid-April, it was quite reasonable for Jesus to see if the tree had any fruit.

The fig tree bore leaves but no fruit. Profession of faith without the reality was always hated by Jesus. Many Jews of Jesus' day made a great show of religion with all their ritual observances but never produced the spiritual qualities God looked for.

Tuesday: Jesus is anointed

What happened:
Mary anoints Jesus' feet: "Mary took about a pint of pure nard, an expensive perfume; she poured it on Jesus' feet. . . . Judas Iscariot objected 'Why wasn't this perfume sold and the money given to the poor? It is worth a year's wages.' . . . 'Leave her alone,' Jesus replied. 'It was intended that she should save this perfume for the day of my burial.'"

Significant detail:
Perfumes were used at burials, not just festivities (John 19:39–40). It was the normal Jewish custom to anoint a body with aromatic

The events of Jesus' final week were dramatic.

EVENTS OF JESUS' FINAL WEEK

Day	Event	Matthew	Mark	Luke	John
Palm Sunday	Jesus rides into Jerusalem	21:1–11	11:1–10	19:29–44	12:12–19
Monday	Jesus curses the fig tree	21:18–19	11:12–14		
Monday	Jesus cleanses the temple	21:12–13	11:15–18		
Tuesday	Jesus' authority challenged	21:23–27	11:27–33	20:1–8	
Tuesday	Jesus teaches in the temple	21:28–23:39	12:1–44	20:9–21:4	
Tuesday	Jesus anointed in Bethany	26:6–13	14:3–9		12:2–11
Wednesday	The plot thickens	26:14–16	14:10–11	22:3–6	
Thursday	The Lord's Supper	26:17–29	14:12–25	22:7–20	13:1–38
Thursday	Jesus comforts disciples				14:1–16:33
Thursday	Jesus prays in Gethsemane	26:36–46	14:32–42	22:40–46	
Thursday p.m./ Friday a.m.	Jesus is arrested and tried	26:47–27:26	14:43–15:15	22:47–23:25	18:2–19:16
Friday	Jesus is crucified	27:27–56	15:16–41	23:26–49	19:17–30
Friday	Jesus is buried	27:57–66	15:42–47	23:50–56	19:31–42

oils before it was laid to rest (Mark 16:1). Jesus links this act with his own burial, which Mary, without realizing it, is anticipating here.

Wednesday: the plot
What happened:
Judas agrees to betray Jesus: "Then Satan entered Judas, called Iscariot, one of the Twelve. And Judas went to the chief priests and the officers of the temple guard and discussed with them how he might betray Jesus."

Significant detail:
The gospel writers only use this expression "Satan entered" twice. Once here and once during the Last Supper: "As soon as Judas took the bread, Satan entered into him" (John 13:27).

Thursday: preparing to eat the Passover
What happened:
"Jesus sent Peter and John saying, 'Go and make preparations for us to eat the Passover.' 'Where do you want us to prepare for it?' they asked. He replied, 'As you enter the city, a man carrying a jar of water will meet you.'"

Significant detail:
A man was carrying a jar of water. Since this was considered to be women's work, it was extremely unusual to find a man carrying a jar of water. Some scholars feel this was used as some kind of secret sign so that Peter and John knew how they were to identify the person Jesus told them to meet.

Praying in Gethsemane
What happened:
Jesus prays on the Mount of Olives: "And being in anguish, [Jesus] prayed more earnestly, and his sweat was like drops of blood falling to the ground."

Significant detail:
This perspiration reflected the great spiritual battle Jesus was waging.

See also: *Jesus' Death*, pp. 48–49.

Jesus' Death

The physical suffering linked to the way Jesus died is not emphasized by the gospel writers. However, it is not ignored. In the first century A.D. everyone knew that crucifixion was an agonizingly painful death.

Pilate has Jesus flogged

After the death sentence had been passed, it was customary for the prisoner to be flogged with a whip which had small pieces of lead or bone tied to its leather thongs: "[Pilate] had Jesus flogged" (Matthew 27:26).

The soldiers mock Jesus

*   "The men who were guarding Jesus began mocking and beating him" (Luke 22:63).
*   "They stripped him (Matthew 27:28)
*   put a scarlet robe on him (Matthew 27:28)
*   then twisted together a crown of thorns and set it on his head (Matthew 27:29).
*   They spit on him (Matthew 27:30).
*   and took the staff and struck him on the head again and again" (Matthew 27:30).

Jesus' cross is carried for him

It is thought that Simon of Cyrene carried the cross-piece of Jesus' cross.

"As they were going out, they met a man from Cyrene, named Simon, and they forced him to carry the cross" (Matthew 27:32).

Jesus is crucified

The Romans used this method of execution for their worst criminals. The lingering death, which sometimes stretched over days, has been described as the most painful method of death ever devised by man.

A simple stake or pole, only a little taller than a person, was hammered into the ground and criminals and prisoners of war were hung on it to die. The Romans reserved the cross, a pole with a horizontal cross-piece, for the execution of criminals who had committed the worst type of crimes. Early tradition claims that Jesus was crucified on this second type of pole.

Archaeologists have discovered an ankle bone of a young man crucified outside Jerusalem in the first century, still with the metal spike in it which was used to nail him to a cross.

Jesus really died

It is not possible to suggest that Jesus never died and that he revived in the cool of the tomb, thus making the whole idea of his resurrection a sham. John makes it very clear in his gospel that Jesus really died on the cross: "When [the soldiers] came to Jesus and found that he was already dead, they did not break his legs. Instead, one of the soldiers pierced Jesus' side with a spear, bringing a sudden flow of blood and water" (John 19:33–34).

The real death of Jesus was the real life for us. The physical death of Jesus indicates that Jesus really did die. The spiritual significance of his death is that we have spiritual life as a result.

The writers of the letters in the New Testament stress the spiritual meaning of the death of Jesus much more than the agony of the physical death.

Crucifixion was an extremely painful form of execution.

Jesus died on the cross so that we might have spiritual life.

Peter

On the tree

"He himself bore our sins in his body on the tree, so that we might die to sins and live for righteousness; by his wounds you have been healed" (1 Peter 2:24).

Why Jesus died

"For Christ died for sins once for all, the righteous for the unrighteous, to bring you to God" (1 Peter 3:18).

The precious blood of Christ

"For you know that it was not with perishable things such as silver or gold that you were redeemed from the empty way of life handed down to you from your forefathers, but with the precious blood of Christ, a lamb without blemish or defect" (1 Peter 1:18–19).

Jesus' sacrifice freed us to enter the kingdom of Heaven.

Paul

Jesus and his sacrifice

"Live a life of love, just as Christ loved us and gave himself up for us as a fragrant offering and sacrifice to God" (Ephesians 5:2).

Jesus, a substitute

"God made [Jesus] who had no sin to be sin for us, so that in him we might become the righteousness of God" (2 Corinthians 5:21).

Faith in the death of Jesus

"God presented [Jesus] as a sacrifice of atonement, through faith in his blood" (Romans 3:25). The "blood" of Jesus means the "death" of Jesus in the New Testament.

The writer of Hebrews

Once for all

"[Jesus] sacrificed for their sins once for all when he offered himself" (Hebrews 7:27).

John

Purification from sin

"The blood of Jesus, his Son, purifies us from all sin" (1 John 1:7).

Freed us from our sins

"To him who loves us and has freed us from our sins by his blood, and has made us to be a kingdom and priests to serve his God and Father— to him be glory and power for ever and ever! Amen!" (Revelation 1:5–6).

Good Friday

Christians refer to the day that Jesus died, not as bad, sad, tragic Friday, but as Good Friday.

See also: *Jesus' Resurrection*: pp. 50–51.

Jesus' Resurrection

ASSESSING THE EVIDENCE

A number of people who openly declared that they were highly skeptical about the resurrection of Jesus have been surprised by what they discovered when they read the gospels for themselves and reflected on the evidence in favor of his resurrection.

The balance of evidence points to the truth of the resurrection.

Who would have stolen the body?

- The authorities: if it was the authorities who stole the body, they only had to produce the body to stop instantly all talk about Jesus being alive.
- The disciples: if the disciples, it meant that they were prepared to die for a lie.
- Thieves: some graves were broken into by robbers who hoped to find valuables they could steal. They would have had to overpower two armed guards who were on the lookout all night.

MATTHEW'S ACCOUNT

"After the Sabbath, at dawn on the first day of the week, Mary Magdalene and the other Mary went to look at the tomb.

There was a violent earthquake, for an angel of the Lord came down from heaven and, going to the tomb, rolled back the stone and sat on it. His appearance was like lightning, and his clothes were white as snow. The guards were so afraid of him that they shook and became like dead men.

The angel said to the women, 'Do not be afraid, for I know that you are looking for Jesus, who was crucified. He is not here; he has risen, just as he said. Come and see the place where he lay. Then go quickly and tell his disciples, "He has risen from the dead and is going ahead of you into Galilee. There you will see him." Now I have told you.'

So the women hurried away from the tomb, afraid yet filled with joy, and ran to tell his disciples. Suddenly Jesus met them. 'Greetings,' he said. They came to him, clasped his feet and worshiped him."

Matthew 28:1–10

MARK'S ACCOUNT

"When the Sabbath was over, Mary Magdalene, Mary the mother of James, and Salome bought spices so that they might go to anoint Jesus' body. Very early on the first day of the week, just after sunrise, they were on their way to the tomb and they asked each other, 'Who will roll the stone away from the entrance of the tomb?'

But when they looked up, they saw that the stone, which was very large, had been rolled away. As they entered the tomb, they saw a young man dressed in a white robe sitting on the right side and they were alarmed.

'Don't be alarmed,' he said. 'You are looking for Jesus the Nazarene, who was crucified. He has risen! He is not here. See the place where they laid him. But go, tell his disciples and Peter, "He is going ahead of you into Galilee. There you will see him, just as he told you".'"

Mark 16:1–8

THE WITNESSES OF JESUS' RESURRECTION

Witness	Bible reference
Mary Magdalene	John 20:10–18
Peter	Luke 24:34
Two disciples traveling to Emmaus	Luke 24:13–31
The ten apostles	John 20:19–24
The eleven apostles	John 20:25–29
Seven disciples by Lake Tiberias	John 21:1–23
Over 500 people at one time	1 Corinthians 15:6
James	1 Corinthians 15:7
People who saw the ascension	Acts 1:3–11
Stephen	Acts 7:55
Paul	1 Corinthians 15:8
John, exiled on Patmos	Revelation 1:10–19

LUKE'S ACCOUNT

"On the first day of the week, very early in the morning, the women took the spices they had prepared and went to the tomb. They found the stone rolled away from the tomb, but when they entered, they did not find the body of the Lord Jesus. While they were wondering about this, suddenly two men in clothes that gleamed like lightning stood beside them. In their fright the women bowed down with their faces to the ground, but the men said to them, 'Why do you look for the living among the dead?'"

Luke 24:1–8

When the women arrived to anoint Jesus' body they found the tomb opened.

JOHN'S ACCOUNT

"Early on the first day of the week, while it was still dark, Mary Magdalene went to the tomb and saw that the stone had been removed from the entrance. So she came running to Simon Peter and the other disciple, the one Jesus loved, and said, 'They have taken the Lord out of the tomb, and we don't know where they have put him!'

So Peter and the other disciple started for the tomb. Both were running, but the other disciple outran Peter and reached the tomb first. He bent over and looked in at the strips of linen lying there but did not go in. Then Simon Peter, who was behind him, arrived and went into the tomb. He saw the strips of linen lying there, as well as the burial cloth that had been around Jesus' head. The cloth was folded up by itself, separate from the linen. Finally the other disciple, who had reached the tomb first, also went inside. He saw and believed."

John 20:1–8

Jesus Will Return

Jesus' coming again taught in the New Testament

There are 1,527 references to the second coming of Jesus in the Old Testament and it is referred to 319 times in the New Testament, although the exact phrase "second coming" is not actually used.

The visible coming again of the Lord Jesus Christ to this world in a personal and visible way is often called the "coming," or in Greek *parousia*.

Jesus' *parousia*

Jesus himself frequently spoke of his own coming again. Paul, James, Peter, and John write about it in their letters.

This "coming" of Jesus is specifically mentioned in several verses:

- "For as in Adam all die, so in Christ will all be made alive. But each in his own turn: Christ, the first fruits; then, when he comes, those who belong to him" (1 Corinthians 15:22–23).
- "For what is our hope, our joy, or the crown in which we will glory in the presence of our Lord Jesus Christ when he comes?" (1 Thessalonians 2:19).
- "May he strengthen your hearts so that you will be blameless and holy in the presence of our God and Father when our Lord Jesus comes with all his holy ones" (1 Thessalonians 3:13).
- "Be patient, then, brothers, until the Lord's coming" (James 5:7).
- "You too, be patient and stand firm, because the Lord's coming is near" (James 5:8).

Famines will be one sign of Jesus' imminent return.

- "We did not follow cleverly invented stories when we told you about the power and coming of our Lord Jesus Christ" (2 Peter 1:16).
- "And now, dear children, continue in him, so that when he appears we may be confident and unashamed before him at his coming" (1 John 2:28).

Jesus' coming again in Matthew, Mark, and Luke

The first three gospels speak about Jesus' return being accompanied by specific signs (Matthew 19:28, 23:39, 24:1–51; Mark 13:24–37; Luke 12:35–48, 21:25–28). From Luke 21:8–12, for example, we are told that the following signs are linked with Jesus' coming:

- wars
- rumors of wars
- revolutions
- earthquakes
- famines
- signs from heaven
- persecution of God's followers.

Jesus' coming again in John's gospel

"And if I go and prepare a place for you, I will come back and take you to be with me that you also may be where I am" (John 14:3).

Jesus' coming again in Acts

The theme of Jesus' coming is introduced at the beginning of Acts. On the occasion of Jesus' ascension this promise is made by two

WORDS USED BY PAUL TO EXPRESS JESUS' COMING AGAIN

Greek word	English word	Example
parousia	Coming or arrival	May your whole spirit, soul and body be kept blameless at the coming of our Lord Jesus Christ. *Thessalonians 5:23*
apocalypsis	Revelation	This will happen when the Lord Jesus is revealed from heaven in blazing fire with his powerful angels. *Thessalonians 1:7*
epiphaneia	Glorious manifestation	Keep this command without spot or blame until the appearing of our Lord Jesus Christ. *Timothy 6:14*

heavenly beings: "Men of Galilee why do you stand here looking into the sky? This same Jesus, who has been taken from you into heaven, will come back in the same way you have seen him go into heaven" (Acts I: II).

Did Paul make a mistake?

Paul sometimes mentions the coming of Jesus as if it were just round the corner. So did he get it wrong? Nearly 2000 years have passed since he wrote, "According to the Lord's own word, we tell you that we who are still alive, who are left till the coming of the Lord, will certainly not precede those who have fallen asleep" (1 Thessalonians 4:15).

The whole of the New Testament teaches that Jesus' followers should be expecting Jesus to return any day—even tomorrow.

Jesus' second coming will be preceded by wars.

So when will Jesus return?

Jesus taught that we do not know the date of his second coming (Matthew 24:36).

Peter said that in God's view of time, one day is like a thousand years (1 Peter 3:8).

We need to be constantly prepared for Jesus' second coming.

Part

3

Introducing Bible People

56–57
The Names for God

58–59
Old Testament People

60–61
Abraham

62–63
Moses

64–65
The Judges

66–67
The Prophets

68–69
David and the Kings

70–71
The Twelve (1)

72–73
The Twelve (2)

74–75
The Pharisees, Jesus' Opponents

76–77
Paul

78–79
New Testament People

The Names for God

God himself cannot be regarded as a Bible "person" in the same way that we think of Abraham or Peter. But the Bible is basically a book about God. One way that God is revealed to us is by the amazing variety of names that are given to him in the Bible.

God as Creator

"God created the world" (Mark 13:19). This is the most explicit statement Jesus made about God being the Creator. (Other verses: Mark 10:6; Matthew 19:4; Acts 14:15; 17:24; 17:29.)

God as Father

The idea of the fatherhood of God is the most characteristic teaching in the New Testament. See: *Teaching about God the Father*, pp. 82–83.

God as King

In Revelation 4:2, God is pictured as a King sitting on "a throne in heaven." See also: Revelation 21:5.

God as Judge

The certainty of God's judgment is assumed in many places in the gospels (Matthew 3:7ff; 7:1–2; 1:22–24; 12:36–37; Luke 3:7ff).

The apostle Paul often mentions the idea of God as Judge (Romans 2:16; 3:6; 14:10).

God as Spirit

"God is spirit, and his worshipers must worship in spirit and truth" (John 4:24).

FIFTEEN HEBREW NAMES FOR GOD IN THE OLD TESTAMENT		
Name of God	**Meaning of name**	**Bible reference**
1. Elohim	The All-Powerful One	Genesis 1:1
2. El (singular)	The Strong One	Exodus 6:3
3. El-Elyon	The Most High God	Genesis 14:18–22
4. El-Shaddai	The All-Sufficient One	Genesis 17:1
5. El-Olam	The Everlasting God	Genesis 21:33
6. Jehovah (Yahweh)	The Self-Existent One	Exodus 3:14
7. Jehovah-Elohim	Lord God, as Creator	Genesis 1:26
8. Jehovah-Jireh	Jehovah will provide	Genesis 22:13–14
9. Jehovah-Rapha	Jehovah who heals	Exodus 15:25
10. Jehovah-Nissi	Jehovah is my Banner	Exodus 17:15
11. Jehovah-Shalom	Jehovah is Peace	Judges 6:24
12. Jehovah-Shammah	Jehovah is there	Ezekiel 48:3
13. Jehovah-Tsidkenu	Jehovah our Righteousness	Jeremiah 33:16
14. Jehovah-Raah	The Lord is my shepherd	Psalm 23:1
15. Jehovah-Sabaoth	The Lord of Hosts:.God's power in time of trouble	Psalm 46:7

The idea of God as father is found throughout the New Testament.

God as Savior

The title is used of God as well as of Jesus in the New Testament: "This is good, and pleases God our Savior" (1 Timothy 2:3). See also Titus 2:10, 13; 3:4; Jude 25.

God as God Most High

This expresses the idea that God is superior to all other gods that people may believe in (Acts 16:17). See also Luke 8:28 and Mark 5:7.

God as God of the patriarchs

God is called "the God of our fathers" (Acts 22:14), as well as the God of Abraham, Isaac and Jacob (Matthew 8:11; 22:32; Mark 12:26–27; Luke 20:37; Acts 3:13; 7:32).

God as Alpha and Omega

The idea behind this name is that the beginning and the end, as well as everything in between, belongs to God (Revelation 1:8; 21:6). The name is also applied to Jesus in Revelation 22:13.

God is the God of all things throughout the Universe.

God is referred to as a judge several times in the New Testament.

ATTRIBUTES OF GOD IN THE NEW TESTAMENT		
Attribute	**Example**	**Bible Reference**
Glory of God	"Stephen . . . saw the glory of God"	Acts 7:55; Matthew 17:1ff; 2 Peter 1:17
Wisdom and knowledge of God	"We speak of God's secret wisdom"	1 Corinthians 2:7; Romans 11:33; Matthew 6:8
Holiness of God	"You have an anointing from the Holy One"	1 John 2:20; 1 Peter 1:16; Revelation 4:8
Righteousness and justice of God	"For in the gospel a righteousness from God is revealed"	Romans 1:17; 3:21–22; Ephesians 4:24
Love of God	"For God so loved the world that he gave his one and only Son"	John 3:16; 1 John 3:17; 4:7–8, 10, 16, 19
Grace of God	"Continue in the grace of God"	Acts 13:43; Romans 3:34; 5:15
Faithfulness of God	"God . . . is faithful"	1 Corinthians 1:9; Hebrews 10:23

Old Testament People

Fifty men and women from the Old Testament are featured here. After each name comes its meaning, a short description, and relevant Bible references.

The first human families

- **Adam** (*mankind*). The first person created.
  - *Genesis 2–3*
- **Eve** (*life*). In disobedience to God she gave Adam the forbidden fruit.
  - *Genesis 2:18–3:20*
- **Cain** (*acquire*). Having had his sacrifice rejected by God, he murdered Abel.
  - *Genesis 4*
- **Abel** (*shepherd*). Cain's brother, whose sacrifice of a lamb God accepted.
  - *Genesis 4*
- **Noah** (*rest*). Built a 450-foot-long ark in obedience to God.
  - *Genesis 5–9*
- **Methuselah** (*man of the javelin*). Oldest man who ever lived: 969 years.
  - *Genesis 5:21–7*
- **Enoch** (*teacher*). Translated: that is, he went to heaven without dying.
  - *Genesis 5:18–24*
- **Job** (*persecuted*). His story of undeserved suffering is in the book of Job.
  - *Job 1–42*
- **Abraham** (*father of many people*). The founder of the Jewish nation.
  - *Genesis 11–25*
- **Isaac** (*laughing*). Abraham's son, father of Jacob and Esau.
  - *Genesis 21–27*
- **Jacob** (*supplanter*). Tricked his brother Esau out of his inheritance.
  - *Genesis 25–35; 42–50*

- **Esau** (*hairy*). Brother of Jacob who founded the nation of Edom.
  - *Genesis 25–8; 32–3*
- **Melchizedek** (*king of righteousness*). Priest and king. Symbolized Jesus.
  - *Genesis 14:18–20*

Egypt and the Exodus

- **Joseph** (*increaser*). Rose from slave to prime minister in Egypt.
  - *Genesis 30–24; 37–50*
- **Aaron** (*enlightened*). Moses' older brother.
  - *Exodus 4–12; 28–29; 32*
- **Moses** (*drawer out*). Israel's greatest prophet and lawgiver.
  - *Exodus 2 and Deuteronomy*
- **Joshua** (*God is salvation*). Led the Israelites into the Promised Land.
  - *Exodus 17; Joshua*

The judges

- **Samson** (*distinguished*). Ruled Israel for 20 years with his superior strength.
  - *Judges 13–16*
- **Gideon** (*great warrior*). Defeated Midianites with 300 men.
  - *Judges 6–8*
- **Ruth** (*companion*). Left her own country to care for her mother-in-law, Naomi.
  - *Ruth*
- **Samuel** (*asked of God*). Anointed Saul and David to be Israel's kings.
  - *1 Samuel 1–4; 7–16*

Israel's first kings

- **Saul** (*asked*). Israel's first king.
  - *1 Samuel 8–31; 2 Samuel 1*
- **David** (*beloved*). Israel's most illustrious king. A man after God's own heart.
  - *1 and 2 Samuel*

The meaning of Abraham's name, "father of many people," was appropriate because he founded the Jewish nation.

- **Jonathan** (*God is given*). Saul's oldest son and David's best friend.
  - ⌁ *1 Samuel 13–14, 18–20*
- **Goliath** (*an exile*). Killed by David.
  - ⌁ *1 Samuel 22*
- **Bathsheba** (*the seventh daughter*). Uriah's husband who later became David's wife.
  - ⌁ *2 Samuel 11–12*
- **Solomon** (*peace*). David's son. Built the Jerusalem temple.
  - ⌁ *1 Kings 1–11; 2 Chronicles 1–9*

Kings and prophets of Judah
(after Judah and Israel divided into two kingdoms)
- **Joash** (*God has given*). Ruled Judah for 40 years; removed Baal worship.
  - ⌁ *2 Kings 11–12*
- **Isaiah** (*salvation of God*). Prophesied faithfully in Jerusalem for 40 years.
  - ⌁ *Isaiah*
- **Ahaz** (*he holds*). Evil king who encouraged Baal worship.
  - ⌁ *2 Kings 16; 2 Chronicles 28*
- **Manasseh** (*causing forgetfulness*). Offered his own son in child sacrifice.
  - ⌁ *2 Kings 21*
- **Zedekiah** (*Jehovah is mighty*). Jerusalem destroyed after his rebellion.
  - ⌁ *Jeremiah 37–9*
- **Jeremiah** (*God is high*). Prophesied to the last five kings of Judah.
  - ⌁ *Jeremiah*
- **Micah** (*who is like God?*). He predicted Bethlehem as the Messiah's birthplace.
  - ⌁ *Micah*

Kings and prophets of Israel
(after Israel and Judah divided into two kingdoms)
- **Jeroboam** (*I the people-multiplied*). Israel's first king.
  - ⌁ *1 Kings 11–14*
- **Ahab** (*father is brother*). Supporter of Baal worship. Very evil king.
  - ⌁ *1 Kings 16; 20–22*

- **Elijah** (*the Lord is my God*). Faithful, outspoken prophet.
  - ⌁ *1 Kings 17–19*
- **Elisha** (*God is Savior*). Healed Naaman's leprosy.
  - ⌁ *2 Kings 2–9*
- **Amos** (*burden-bearer*). Prophesied against Israel's moral corruption.
  - ⌁ *Amos*
- **Jonah** (*dove*). Prophet who tried to run away from God's call.
  - ⌁ *Jonah*

After slaying Goliath, David became Israel's most illustrious king.

Exile and return from exile
- **Nebuchadnezzar** (*may the god Nebo defend the boundary*). Babylon's king.
  - ⌁ *Daniel 1–4*
- **Ezekiel** (*strengthens*). Prophesied to exiles in Babylon.
  - ⌁ *Ezekiel*
- **Daniel** (*God is my judge*). Thrown into lions' den.
  - ⌁ *Daniel*
- **Cyrus** (*no known meaning*). Allowed exiled Jews to return to Jerusalem.
  - ⌁ *Ezra 1–6*
- **Nehemiah** (*the Lord comforts*). Led Jews back to Jerusalem. Rebuilt walls.
  - ⌁ *Nehemiah*
- **Ezra** (*the Lord helps*). Led second group of Jews back to Jerusalem.
  - ⌁ *Ezra*
- **Esther** (*myrtle*). Heroine of the book named after her.
  - ⌁ *Esther*
- **Haggai** (*born on a feast day*). Told returned exiles to rebuild the temple.
  - ⌁ *Haggai*
- **Malachi** (*my messenger*). Attacked empty ritual worship held in the temple.
  - ⌁ *Malachi*
- **Zechariah** (*the Lord remembers*). Accused returned exiles of spiritual apathy.
  - ⌁ *Zechariah*

Abraham

The City of Ur

Abraham grew up in Ur, a city on the banks of the River Euphrates in Southern Mesopotamia. He was born around 2166 B.C. in the middle of the Bronze Age. Until 2000 B.C., Ur was one of the chief cities of southern Mesopotamia. It was vastly wealthy and powerful, though it was not big by today's standards—only around half a square mile in size. But it had schools, libraries, and a large temple to the mood god.

Sir Leonard Woolley

In 1923 Sir Leonard Woolley discovered the royal cemetery where the kings and queens of Ur were buried. When a king or queen died, they were put in a small stone room underground with all their clothes and jewelry. Then their servants, their musicians, their attendants, and their guards followed them down. They even took their carts and cattle. They were ready, they thought, to look after the king and queen in the future life. They drank poison and died.

GOD SAID TO ABRAHAM

"Leave your country, your people and
your father's household and go to
the land I will show you.

"I will make you into a great nation
and I will bless you;
I will make your name great,
and you will be a blessing.
I will bless those who bless you,
and whoever curses you I will curse;
and all the peoples on earth
will be blessed through you."

Genesis 12:1–3

FACTFILE ON ABRAHAM

Name: **Abram (later changed
to Abraham)**
Meaning: **Both names mean
"Father of many people"**
Born: **c. 2166 B.C.**
Home: **Ur, then Haran, then Canaan**
Father: **Terah**
Wives: **Sarai (Sarah), Keturah**
Concubine: **Hagar**
Famous for: **His trust in God**
Accomplishment: **Founded nation of Israel**
Known as: **Father of the Jews**

*Abraham left the city of his birth
to become a nomad before
settling in Canaan.*

HIS NOMADIC EXISTENCE

"Leave your country"

Abraham left his comfortable town life in Ur to live a traveling life like a nomad. He took his father, Terah, his wife Sarah, and his nephew Lot. On the way they stopped at Haran, where his father died.

Canaan

Abraham traveled 625 miles from Haran to Shechem, a famous holy place in the highlands of central Canaan. There Abraham built an altar and claimed the pagan place for God.

God said to him, "To your offspring I will give this land" (Genesis 12:7).

GOD'S PROMISES
TO ABRAHAM

God's covenant with Abraham

God made a covenant, or agreement, with Abraham.

In this covenant He promised Abraham three things:

- I will make a great nation from your descendants.
- I will give you this land of Canaan.
- You will be famous, and people all over the world will bless one another, using your name.

God also promised that Abraham would have a son by Sarah, who would be the mother of the nations.

Circumcision

In the covenant, God told Abraham to circumcise all the men in his camp. Circumcision was common in Abraham's time among other nations, but God gave it a special meaning for Abraham and his descendants.

It was to be the outward sign of Abraham's commitment to God, whom he would trust and serve: "You are to undergo circumcision, and it will be the sign of the covenant between me and you" (Genesis 17:11).

Melchizedek

Melchizedek, one of the Bible's most mysterious people, was a priest-king who ruled over the city of Salem, later called Jerusalem. After the battle of the five kings, Melchizedek came to meet Abraham with gifts of food and wine. He blessed Abraham,

Abraham's descendants became the nation of Israel.

MAJOR COVENANTS IN THE OLD TESTAMENT

With Noah	*Genesis 9:8–17*
With Abraham	*Genesis 15:9–21*
At Sinai	*Exodus 19–24*
With Phinehas	*Numbers 25:10–31*
With David	*2 Samuel 7:5–16*
The new covenant	*Jeremiah 31:31–34*

and Abraham gave him a tenth of all his victory spoils. So Abraham saw that though Melchizedek was a Canaanite, amazingly, he was a priest of the true God. In future years Bible writers were to compare him to Jesus (Genesis 14:17–20; Psalm 110:4; Hebrews 6:20–7:28).

Abraham's obedience

Some years after God had miraculously enabled Sarah and Abraham to have a son, even though Sarah was well past the normal age for having a baby, God ordered Abraham to sacrifice Isaac as a burnt offering (Genesis 22:2).

But at the last moment, God said, "Do not lay a hand on the boy . . . Now I know that you fear God" (Genesis 22:12).

Moses

LIFE IN EGYPT

As a baby, Moses was discovered in a reed basket in the River Nile among the bullrushes. Pharaoh's daughter brought the Hebrew baby up as her own and as an Egyptian prince

When Moses grew up, he "refused to be known as the son of Pharaoh's daughter. He chose to be mistreated along with the people of God" (Hebrews 11:24–25). After he had killed a cruel Egyptian taskmaster, he escaped to Midian, where he married Zipporah and became a shepherd.

BY FAITH

"By faith Moses, when he had grown up, refused to be known as the son of Pharaoh's daughter. He chose to be mistreated along with the people of God rather than to enjoy the pleasures of sin for a short time.

He regarded disgrace for the sake of Christ as of greater value than the treasures of Egypt, because he was looking ahead to his reward.

By faith he left Egypt, not fearing the king's anger; he persevered because he saw him who is invisible.

By faith he kept the Passover and the sprinkling of blood, so that the destroyer of the firstborn would not touch the firstborn of Israel.

By faith the people passed through the Red Sea as on dry land; but when the Egyptians tried to do so, they were drowned."

Hebrews 11:24–29

The Israelites spent forty years in the desert before arriving in the promised land.

The great escape

God called Moses back to Egypt through the remarkable event of the burning bush in the desert. With his brother, Aaron, as his spokesman, God charged Moses with the task of leading the Israelites out of their slavery in Egypt. The Egyptian Pharaoh refused to let the Israelites go and nine devastating plagues followed. Then after the tenth plague, in which all the firstborn Egyptian sons died, Pharaoh allowed the Israelites to leave.

FORTY YEARS IN THE DESERT

At Mount Sinai God gave Moses the Ten Commandments, as well as detailed instructions about how the tabernacle should be built.

For forty years, Moses led an often rebellious people through the desert. He died without entering, but within sight of, the Promised Land.

The tabernacle: God dwells among his people

In the wilderness wanderings, God provided through Moses the Ten Commandments and other laws and a way to worship God in the tabernacle, a very special tent. The tabernacle became the basis for Israel's future worship of God in the temple.

Moses was a faithful
leader of his people.

THE TEN COMMANDMENTS

- You shall have no other gods besides me.
- You shall not worship any idol.
- You shall not misuse the name of the Lord your God.
- Remember the Sabbath day by keeping it holy.
- Honor your father and mother.
- You shall not murder.
- You shall not commit adultery.
- You shall not steal.
- You shall not give false testimony against your neighbor.
- You shall not covet anything that belongs to your neighbor.

from Exodus 20:1–17

A STUDY GUIDE: TEN KEY PASSAGES ON THE LIFE OF MOSES

Bible Passage	Key Theme
Exodus 1–2	Background on Moses' life. The oppression of the Israelites and the birth of Moses.
Exodus 3–4	Moses and the burning bush. Moses hesitates about accepting God's call.
Exodus 5:22–6:12	Moses is frustrated when Pharaoh increases the workload of the Israelites.
Exodus 7–11	Moses' confrontations with Pharaoh.
Exodus 16	The Israelites ignore Moses.
Exodus 32	Moses discovers the Israelites indulging in pagan worship.
Numbers 14	Moses deals with the rebellion at Kadesh Barnea.
Numbers 27	Moses seeks God's guidance.
Deuteronomy 11	Moses speaks of God's reasons in calling his people to obey the law.
Deuteronomy 32	The song of Moses. Moses teaches this song to strengthen Israel's faith.

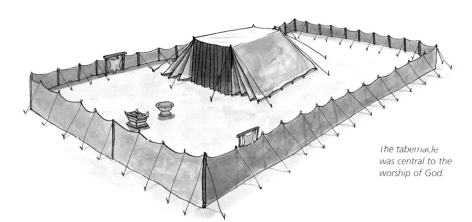

The tabernacle
was central to the
worship of God.

The Judges

This period in Israel's history is aptly summed up several times in the book of Judges in the same way: "In those days Israel had no king; everyone did as he saw fit" (Judges 17:6; 21:25).

The times of the judges is sometimes called the "Dark Ages" of the history of Israel.

Liberators

As far as the Israelites were concerned, the judges were liberators. From the death of Joshua to the arrival of Samuel, God gave the Israelites military leaders who rescued them from their enemies in the land of Canaan.

A depressing cycle

The events during the times of the judges can be summarized as: "Sin–oppression–prayer–deliverance–peace."

Sin

The Israelites turn from God. Instead of trusting in God, they worship the gods of Canaan: "The Israelites cried out to the LORD, 'We have sinned against you, forsaking our God and serving the Baals'" (Judges 10:10).

Oppression

A foreign enemy defeats and oppresses the Israelites.

Prayer

The Israelites turn back to God in repentance and prayer.

Deliverance

God sends a deliverer/judge to rescue the Israelites.

Peace

The Israelites enjoy a period of peace, until they are unfaithful to God again, renewing the cycle.

ISRAEL'S JUDGES			
Name of Judge	Years ruled	Enemy or Place of origin	Reference in Book of Judges
Othniel	40	Nomads	3:5–11
Ehud	80	Moabites	3:12–30
Shamgar	unknown	Philistines	3:31
Deborah	40	Canaanites	4–5
Gideon	40	Midianites	6:11–8:33
Tola	23	From Issachar	10:1–2
Jair	22	From Gilead	10:3–5
Jephthah	6	Ammonites	10:6–12:7
Ibzan	7	From Bethlehem	12:8–10
Elon	10	From Zebulun	12:11–12
Abdon	8	From Ephraim	12:13–15
Samson	20	Philistines	13–16

IDOLATRY

Canaanite religion

The Canaanites practiced fertility worship. This involved especially honoring the Master (Baal) and his Mistress. In practice this meant that the Canaanite priests and priestesses in their temples had sexual intercourse with the Canaanites as part of their ritual of worship. To any right-minded Israelite, this was clearly wrong and idolatrous.

The Ras Shamra epic

The Ras Shamra religious epic, discovered in Ugarit in northern Syria on thousands of clay tablets, provides sordid details about the Canaanite fertility cults which were more degrading than others that took place in the ancient world.

The immoral gods, serpents, prostitute goddesses, cultic doves, and bulls frequently won the hearts of the Israelites.

Gideon destroys an altar to Baal

Gideon (Judges 6–8) is presented as the ideal judge. His first job was to purge his father's house of idolatry. Gideon was nearly stoned for his pains by the worshipers of Baal. But Gideon's father, Joash, "replied to the hostile crowd around him, 'Are you going to plead Baal's cause? Are you trying to save him?

The Israelites were often drawn to the pagan deities of the Canaanite fertility cults.

SAMSON'S STRENGTHS AND WEAKNESSES

Strengths

Separated by a Nazarite vow *Judges 13:5*

At times, spiritual *Judges 13:25*

Physically strong *Judges 14:5–6; 15:14–15 2*

Weaknesses

Looked for evil companion *Judges 14:1–4*

At times, full of lust *Judges 16:1–4*

Weak in temptation *Judges 16:15–17*

Whoever fights for him shall be put to death by morning! If Baal really is a god, he can defend himself when someone breaks down his altar.' So that day they called Gideon 'Jerub-Baal,' saying, 'Let Baal contend with him,' because he broke down Baal's altar" (Judges 6:31–32).

Samson

Greater attention is paid to Samson (Judges 13–16) than to any other judge before the time of Samuel. A number of his exploits may embarrass us, but they should be seen set against the background of the dark days of the time. For all Samson's failings, the writer to the Hebrews remembers positive things about Samson's life, "who through faith conquered kingdoms, administered justice, and gained what was promised" (Hebrews 11:33).

Today many people still fall into the trap of worshiping other things instead of God.

The Prophets

Elijah

The only personal piece of information one can glean from the Bible about Elijah is that he was a "Tishbite, from Tishbe in Gilead" (1 Kings 17:1).

Elijah's ministry as a prophet is recorded in 1 Kings 17–19; 21 and 2 Kings 1–2. Elijah's ministry is presented in six parts:

- his prediction of a drought
- the contest on Mount Carmel
- his flight to Horeb
- the Naboth incident
- the oracle about Ahaziah
- his translation in a fiery chariot.

The first part of Elijah's ministry was his prediction of drought.

With the exception of his translation, Elijah's life was dominated by the battle between the worship of the god of Baal and the worship of Yahweh. He was persecuted for denouncing Ahab and Jezebel (1 Kings 17–21:21; 2 Kings 1–2:18).

Elijah is mentioned more than 30 times in the New Testament, and both John the Baptist and Jesus were mistaken for Elijah. During the Transfiguration, Jesus was seen by the apostles Peter, James, and John talking with Moses and Elijah. Peter offered to make tabernacles for them (Matthew 17:1–4).

Elijah arrived with a fiery message, and he left the earth's stage in a chariot of fire.

ELISHA'S MIRACLES (2 KINGS)

- Dividing the Jordan   2:14
- Healing the waters   2:21–22
- The judgment over irreverence 2:23–24
- Valleys filled with water 3:9–24
- The widow's oil 4:1–7
- Raising of the Shunammite's son 4:32–36
- Poisonous stew made wholesome 4:38–41
- Feeding a crowd   4:42–44
- Healing General Naaman   5:1–14
- Gehazi struck with leprosy   5:26–27
- The floating axe-head   6:5–7
- Making the Syrians go blind   6:15–23
- Foretelling the Syrians' defeat   7
- Resurrection from his bones   13:20–21

MAJOR AND MINOR PROPHETS

5 MAJOR PROPHETS
- Isaiah
- Daniel
- Lamentations (of Jeremiah)
- Jeremiah
- Ezekiel

12 MINOR PROPHETS
- Hosea
- Amos
- Jonah
- Nahum
- Zephaniah
- Zechariah
- Joel
- Obadiah
- Micah
- Habakkuk
- Haggai
- Malachi

ORAL PROPHETS
- Nathan
- Idoo
- Elisha
- Oded
- Azariah
- Jahaziel
- Ahijah
- Jehu
- Elijah
- Shemaiah
- Hanani
- Huldah

HOW THE PROPHET JEREMIAH WAS TREATED

Event	Reference in Jeremiah
He was rejected	11:18–21
His friends mistreated him	12:2–6
He argued with false prophets face to face	14:13–16
He exposed the false prophet Hananiah	28:10–17
He was beaten and put in the stocks	20:1–2
His life was threatened	26:8; 36:26
He was imprisoned	32:2–3; 37:11–15
Some of his prophecies were burned	36:22–25
He was put in a cistern and left to die	38:6
He was bound in chains	40:1

Many prophets left no written record of their prophecies, but are known as "oral prophets."

Elisha

Elisha was Elijah's assistant and disciple. He worked for 55 years through the reigns of Joram, Jehu, Jehoahaz, and Joash.

Elisha prayed that when Elijah was taken up to heaven, he would receive a double portion of Elijah's spirit (2 Kings 2:9).

Elisha's ministry was characterized by his fourteen miracles.

Elisha anticipated Jesus' ministry of miracles. Elisha is mentioned once in the New Testament, "And there were many in Israel with leprosy in the time of Elisha the prophet, yet not one of them was cleansed—only Naaman the Syrian" (Luke 4:27).

PROPHETS AND THEIR WRITINGS

There are 17 books in the Old Testament which are called the books of the prophets. The first five books of the prophets are sometimes called the "major" prophets. The next 12 books of prophecies are sometimes called the "minor" prophets, not because they are unimportant, but because as written records they are much shorter than the first four books.

In addition to these, there were prophets who left no surviving records. These are sometimes called "oral" prophets.

Characteristics of the prophets

They were also called: seers, watchmen, men of God, messengers, and servants of the Lord.

The most frequently used title is prophet (nabi), used over 300 times, which refers to someone who had been appointed or called to proclaim God's message.

Jeremiah

Very few personal details are known about many of the Old Testament prophets. But in the case of Jeremiah we know the above ten personal consequences of his preaching.

See also: *Prophetic Books of the Old Testament (1 and 2)*, pp. 118–121.

David and the Kings

KINGS GALORE

There were 42 kings and 1 queen of Israel and Judah. So it is hardly surprising that reading the seemingly endless exploits of the kings of Israel and Judah in 1 and 2 Kings and 2 Chronicles can be confusing.

It helps to keep certain things in mind.

First, the three kings of Israel while Israel was a single kingdom were Saul, David, and Solomon. Israel's capital was Jerusalem.

Second, Israel split into two kingdoms after Solomon reigned:

- The northern kingdom retained the name Israel; Israel's capital was Samaria.
- The southern kingdom was called Judah; Judah's capital was Jerusalem.

Third, the divided kingdoms were defeated by foreign powers at different times:

- Israel fell to Assyria in 722 B.C. after a long siege of Samaria.
- Judah fell to Babylonia in 586 B.C. after the siege of Jerusalem.

The rise and fall of King Saul

Saul's rise

- Israel demands a king, to be like the other nations.
  - *1 Samuel 8*
- Saul is chosen and anointed by Samuel.
  - *1 Samuel 9–10*
- Saul's leadership is confirmed and he successfully delivers a city.
  - *1 Samuel 11*

Saul's fall

- Saul desecrates the priesthood by offering up a sacrifice.
  - *1 Samuel 13*
- Saul becomes jealous of David and hunts him as if he were a wild animal.
  - *1 Samuel 23–24*
- Saul orders the priests of God to be killed.
  - *1 Samuel 22*

- Saul visits the witch of Endor.
  - *1 Samuel 28*

King Solomon

King Solomon is remembered for being:

- wise
- wealthy
- building the temple
- not being completely faithful to God.

King Solomon was known for building the temple in Jerusalem.

DAVID

King David

King David was Israel's second and greatest king and ruled for 40 years.

David's story is found from 1 Samuel 16 to 1 Kings 2, with much of the material paralleled in 1 Chronicles 2–29.

David was:

- a man after God's heart
  - *1 Samuel 13:14*
- courageous
  - *1 Samuel 17:34–36*
- an accomplished soldier who became king in Jerusalem
  - *2 Samuel 5:7*
- compassionate toward the disadvantaged Mephibosheth
  - *2 Samuel 9*
- an adulterer and murderer
  - *2 Samuel 11*
- capable of sincere repentance.
  - *2 Samuel 12; Psalm 51*

David was a great king, but had a flawed character.

David's importance in the New Testament

- There are 58 references to David in the New Testament.
- An often-repeated title given to Jesus was "Son of David."
- Paul writes, "as to his human nature [Jesus] was a descendant of David" (Romans 1:3).
- John records that Jesus said, "I am the Root and the Offspring of David" (Revelation 22:16).

KINGS OF ISRAEL

KINGS OF THE SINGLE KINGDOM OF ISRAEL

Saul • David • Solomon

KINGS OF THE DIVIDED KINGDOM

Judah	Israel
• Rehoboam	• Jeroboam I
• Abijam	• Nadab
• Asa	• Baasha
• Jehoshaphat	• Elah
• Jehoram	• Zimri
• Ahaziah	• Omri
• Athaliah (queen)	• Ahab
• Joash	• Ahazia
• Amaziah	• Jehoram
• Uzziah	• Jehu
• Jotham	• Jehoahaz
• Ahaz	• Jehoash
• Hezekiah	• Jeroboam II
• Manasseh	• Zechariah
• Amon	• Shallum
• Josiah	• Menahem
• Jehoahaz	• Pekahiah
• Jehoiakim	• Pekah
• Jehoiachin	• Hoshea
• Zedekiah	

As a young man, David looked after his father, Jesse's sheep in Bethlehem.

ANOINTING

The tabernacle and all its furniture had olive oil poured over them to mark them out for God's special use. Kings, prophets, and priests were also anointed with oil.

Samuel anointed Saul and David to be kings of Israel. They were, in Hebrew, "messiah-ed," or, in Greek, "christ-ed."

Jesus was the "Messiah" or "Christ." He was the anointed one, the one specially chosen by God.

Animals' horns were used for storing anointing oil: "The LORD said to Samuel, 'How long will you mourn for Saul, since I have rejected him as king over Israel? Fill your horn with oil and be on your way; I am sending you to Jesse of Bethlehem. I have chosen one of his sons to be king'" (1 Samuel 16:1).

Psalm 89:20 says: "I have found David my servant; with my sacred oil I have anointed him".

The Twelve (1)

THE DISCIPLES

Jesus had many loyal friends and faithful followers, such as Lazarus and his sisters, Mary and Martha, but they were not among his special disciples who accompanied him on his three-year ministry of teaching and healing.

After spending a whole night in prayer (Luke 6:12), Jesus chose twelve disciples.

THE TWELVE

- Simon (called Peter)
- Andrew
- James (brother of John)
- John
- Philip
- Bartholomew
- Thomas
- Matthew
- James (son of Alphaeus)
- Judas (whose surname was Thaddaeus)
- Simon (the Zealot)
- Judas Iscariot

Matthew 10:1–4; Mark 3:13–19; Luke 6:12–16

Why not 11 or 13?

Jesus' twelve disciples became known as "The Twelve."

They were frequently referred to by this name, and are called "The Twelve" 3 times in Matthew's gospel, 8 times in Mark's gospel, 6 times in Luke's gospel, and 4 times in John's gospel: "Jesus arrived with the Twelve" (Mark 14:17).

The gospels do not record why Jesus appointed 12 disciples, rather than eleven or thirteen or another number. However, throughout the Bible numbers are highly significant and often extremely symbolic.

Simon, Peter, Andrew, James, and John were fishing partners on the Sea of Galilee.

There were twelve tribes of Israel, and the twelve apostles and twelve tribes of Israel are mentioned in very close proximity in at least one place in the Bible.

Describing his vision of the new Jerusalem, John writes, "It had a great, high wall with twelve gates, and with twelve angels at the gates. On the gates were written the names of the twelve tribes of Israel. . . The wall of the city had twelve foundations, and on them were the names of the twelve apostles of the Lamb" (Revelation 21:12, 14).

It is assumed from this that the number twelve emphasizes the link between the Old Testament people of God and the New Testament church.

Teenagers

One fact about the apostles that has been obscured by most artistic impressions of the Twelve is their age. They must have been a lot younger than most people would imagine. If most of them lived until the last quarter of the first century, and John into the second century, they must have been teenagers when Jesus called them.

Jesus sometimes joined the apostles on fishing trips.

THE APOSTLES

Apostles

"[Jesus] called his disciples to him and chose twelve of them, whom he also designated apostles" (Luke 6:13).

The word "apostle" comes from the Greek verb meaning "to send." The English word "missionary" comes from a Latin word with the same meaning. Apostles were people sent out, commissioned for a particular task (Luke 6:14–16). The apostles were Jesus' appointed representatives.

Simon, called Peter

- Brother of Andrew, who brought him to meet Jesus initially, and a fisherman on Lake Galilee.
- He had spiritual insight. He could say, "You are the Christ, the Son of the living God" (Matthew 16:15).
- He was inconsistent. A few verses after declaring that Jesus was Christ, Jesus had to rebuke Peter: "Get behind me Satan! You are a stumbling block to me" (Matthew 16:23).
- A witness to Jesus' death. He wrote in the first of his two letters, "I appeal as a . . . witness of Christ's sufferings" (1 Peter 5:1).
- He denied Jesus three times within hours of saying, "Even if I have to die with you, I will never disown you" (Mark 14:31).
- After Jesus' resurrection he became a fearless preacher (Acts 2:14–40).

- According to the historian Eusebius, Peter was crucified in Rome, probably during Emperor Nero's reign.

The names of Simon

He had four names:

- *Simeon*: his Hebrew name, meaning "hearing."
- *Simon*: a Greek form of Simeon.
- *Cephas*: Aramaic for "rock."
- *Peter*: Greek for "rock."

This disciple was most often called "Peter" by the New Testament writers.

Andrew

- Brought his brother and fellow fisherman, Peter, to meet Jesus. He told Peter, "We have found the 'Messiah' (that is, the Christ). And he brought him to Jesus" (John 1:41–42).
- Andrew found a boy with five loaves and two fish for the feeding of the 5,000 (John 6:8–9).

James (brother of John)

- James, with his brother John (sons of a fisherman, Zebedee), were fishing partners on Lake Galilee with Peter and Andrew (Luke 5:7–10.)
- With Peter and John, James was one of Jesus' inner circle of three people who were the only people to witness certain events, like the Transfiguration

See also: *The Twelve (2)*, pp. 72–73.

Twelve was a significant number in the Bible: there were also twelve tribes of Israel.

The Twelve (2)

John

- The brother of James. He was not a lone fisherman on Lake Galilee, but helped to run a family business in the fish trade (Mark 1:20).
- John tried to stop a man from driving out demons in the name of Jesus, because he was not one of Jesus' disciples. Jesus told him not to do this (Mark 9:38–41).
- It has been said that he was the only disciple who dared to stand at the foot of Jesus' cross as he died. What is certain is that Jesus committed his mother Mary to be looked after by John (John 19:25–27).
- In his own gospel, he never mentions himself or his brother James by name, but refers to himself as "the disciple whom Jesus loved" (John 13:23; 19:26; 20:2; 21:7, 20–24).
- John is sometimes known as the "apostle of love" because of his insistence in his gospel and letters that Christians love God and each other. "Dear friends, let us love one another, for love comes from God. Everyone who loves has been born of God and knows God. . . Dear friends, since God so loved us, we also ought to love one another" (1 John 4:7, 11).

Philip

- When Philip (not to be confused with the evangelist of the same name in Acts 21:8) was called by Jesus to follow him, Philip was on his own. He was not called as one

THE BOOKS OF JOHN

Gospel of John

John 1

John 2

John 3

The Book of Revelation

of a pair, as most of the other disciples were (John 1:43).
- When 5,000 people came together to listen to Jesus, Philip asked where they could obtain food to feed them, as, "Eight months' wages would not buy enough bread for each one to have a bite!" (John 6:7).
- During the Last Supper, Philip said to Jesus, "Lord, show us the Father and that will be enough for us" (John 14:8). Jesus told him that they had already seen the Father in him.

Bartholomew

- He is called Bartholomew by Matthew, Mark, and Luke, but Nathaniel by John (John 1:45).
- Apart from Jesus initially calling Bartholomew to follow him, and calling him "a true Israelite, in whom there is nothing false" (John 1:47), we know nothing about him.

Thomas

- Thomas is called Didymus (John 20:24), meaning the Twin. The gospels reveal nothing about his call to follow Jesus or his family background.
- His understanding and faith may not always have been strong, but he was prepared to die for Jesus, on at least one occasion: "Let us also go, that we may die with him" (John 11:16).
- In the upper room, Jesus said to his disciples that they knew the way to the place he was going. But Thomas complained, "Lord, we don't know where you are going, so how can we know the way?" Jesus answered, "I am the way . . ." (John 14:4–6).
- Thomas will forever be remembered as Doubting Thomas because he did not believe the other disciples when they said that they had seen Jesus alive after his crucifixion (John 20:25).

- When confronted by the risen Lord Jesus himself, Thomas responded with wholehearted worship and said, "My Lord and my God!" (John 20:28).

Matthew

- In response to the words "Follow me" (Matthew 9:9), Matthew got up and followed Jesus and left his tax collector's booth for good.
- Because Matthew, called Levi by Luke, was able to hold "a great banquet for Jesus at his house" (Luke 5:29) to which a large crowd of tax collectors and others also came, it is assumed that Matthew was well off.
- Matthew is the traditional author of the gospel which bears his name.

Matthew the tax collector

If you wanted to insult somebody in the New Testament, you called him or her a "tax collector."

The three groups of people often linked together in the gospels as people whom everyone despised were prostitutes, sinners, and tax collectors (Matthew 21:31). No self-respecting Jew associated with a tax collector.

James (son of Alphaeus)

- The only unambiguous reference to this James comes in the three lists of the Twelve.
- Some have speculated that this James was the brother of Matthew as both are called "the son of Alphaeus."

Judas (whose surname was Thaddaeus)

- John 14:22 identifies this Judas as "not Judas Iscariot" so that he would not be confused with Judas the betrayer of Jesus. He is not to be confused either with Judas, Jesus' brother (Matthew 13:55), or with Judas of Galilee (Acts 5:37).

- The only thing we know about him is that he asked Jesus this question in the upper room: "But, Lord, why do you intend to show yourself to us and not to the world" (John 14:22).

Simon (the Zealot)

- Luke calls him "Simon who was called the Zealot" (Luke 6:15), as do Mark and Matthew. Because of this, some think that Simon was a member of the Jewish resistance movement.
- The gospels do not record how Jesus called Simon the Zealot to be one of his followers.

Judas Iscariot

- Judas was the treasurer for the Twelve. "Judas had charge of the money" (John 13:29).
- The gospel writers give details about how Judas planned Jesus' betrayal (Matthew 26:14–16; Mark 14:10–11; Luke 22:3–6; John 13:27–30).
- They also record how this was carried out (John 18:2–6).
- Matthew is the only gospel to record Judas' suicide by hanging (Matthew 27:1–10). But Luke (Acts 1:18–19) also records the event.
- The apostles chose Matthias "to take over this apostolic ministry, which Judas left to go where he belongs" (Acts 1:25).

The Pharisees, Jesus' Opponents

AN IMPORTANT JEWISH SECT

Pharisees

- Their name means "the separated ones."
- They were the most important Jewish sect in Jesus' day, numbering around 5,000.
- They believed that their detailed descriptions about how to keep the law, also known as their oral traditions, were as important as the law that was given by Moses.
- They believed that they were the only righteous Jews alive, since only they kept all the meticulous details of the law.
- Jesus came into conflict with them often and pointed out to them that their loveless attitude to religion meant that they were breaking the spirit of the law all the time, no matter how careful they were about keeping the letter of the law.
- They were meticulous over such issues as tithing and ceremonial washings.

Jesus exposes the Pharisees

"You have let go of the commands of God and are holding on to the traditions of men" (Mark 7:8).

PARABLES

Parables told against the Pharisees and the teachers of the law

It is often surprising to note that some of Jesus' most famous parables were originally told as a result of hostility from the Pharisees and the teachers of the law.

The Pharisees were often criticized by Jesus for their hypocrisy.

As an introduction to Jesus' three parables about the lost sheep, the lost coin, and the lost son, Luke writes, "Now the tax collectors and 'sinners' were all gathering round to hear [Jesus]. But the Pharisees and the teachers of the law muttered, 'This man welcomes sinners and eats with them" (Luke 15:1–2).

A question from "an expert in the law" prompted Jesus to tell his famous parable of the Good Samaritan (Luke 10:25–29).

After the parable of the tenants, "the teachers of the law and the chief priests looked for a way to arrest [Jesus] immediately, because they knew he had spoken this parable against them" (Luke 20:19).

Good Pharisees

Not all Pharisees were bad. It appears that the leading Pharisee, Nicodemus, became a follower of Jesus.

TEN PARABLES AIMED AT THE PHARISEES AND TEACHERS OF LAW

- The parable of the lost sheep
  - *Luke 15:3–7.*
- The parable of the lost coin
  - *Luke 15:8–10.*
- The parable of the lost son
  - *Luke 15:11–32.*
- The two debtors *Luke 7:41–43.*
- The Good Samaritan *Luke 10:30–37.*
- Choosing places of honor at a wedding feast *Luke 14:7–14.*
- The great banquet and reluctant guests
  - *Luke 14:16–24.*
- The Pharisee and the tax collector
  - *Luke 18:10–14.*
- The parable of the tenants
  - *Luke 20:9–16.*
- The two sons *Matthew 21:28–31.*

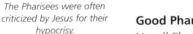

In the early church, some believers . . . "belonged to the party of the Pharisees" (Acts 15:5).

Paul once said, "I am a Pharisee, the son of a Pharisee" (Acts 23:6). See also Philippians 3:5.

The Sadducees

- The Sadducees, or "righteous ones," were a Jewish sect mainly made up of priests, from 166 B.C.–A.D. 70.
- They are mentioned twelve times in the New Testament. They were opponents of the Pharisees, but nevertheless joined forces with them against Jesus.
- They believed in the Mosaic law, which they interpreted even more literally than the Pharisees did, and only accepted the first five books of the Bible as part of the canon of Scripture.
- They rejected the oral law or traditions of men.
- Unlike the Pharisees, they did not believe in the resurrection, in angels, or in spirits (Acts 23:8).
- They had enormous influence because the High Priest was chosen from among their ranks.
- They were the most powerful force in the Sanhedrin, the highest Jewish court, which the High Priest chaired.

EXPOSURE

Jesus exposes the Pharisees and the teachers of the law

- "Woe to you, teachers of the law and Pharisees, you hypocrites! You give a tenth of your spices—mint, dill and cummin. But you have neglected the more important matters of the law—justice, mercy, and faithfulness" (Matthew 23:23).
- "You clean the outside of the cup and dish, but inside they are full of greed and self-indulgence" (Matthew 23:25).

JESUS EXPOSES THE TEACHERS OF THE LAW

"Watch out for the teachers of the law. They like to walk around in flowing robes and be greeted in the market-places, and have the most important seats in the synagogues and the places of honor at the banquets. They devour widows' houses and for a show make lengthy prayers. Such men will be punished most severely."

Mark 12:38–40

Teachers of the law

- They were made up of people who copied, studied, and taught the Jewish law.
- Like the Pharisees, they accepted the authority of oral traditions.
- They acted as lawyers and judges in the days of the New Testament.

The Pharisees' outward appearance of piety hid an inner lack of spirituality.

OTHER PARTIES IN THE NEW TESTAMENT

Herodians

- They were a Jewish party who supported the Roman authorities and King Herod.
- They tried to trap Jesus with their question, "Is it right to pay taxes to Caesar or not?" (Matthew 22:15–22).

Zealots

They were devoted to gaining Israel's independence from Rome and used violent methods if necessary.

Assassins

These were the most extreme of the Zealots. Paul was once mistaken for being one (Acts 21:38).

Paul

FROM PERSECUTOR TO PERSECUTED

Paul was converted to Christ on the road to Damascus.

Saul was a fanatical Pharisee until his dramatic conversion to Christ, after which, with the name Paul, he became a pioneer missionary and the leading Christian theologian of his day. His letters account for about a quarter of the New Testament.

Paul's "lost" letters

We do not have all the letters Paul wrote.

There are four references to his "lost" letters.

- 1 Corinthians 5:9
- 2 Corinthians 19:9–10
- Colossians 4:16
- 2 Thessalonians 3:17

Summary of Paul's life before his public ministry

- Born a Roman citizen in Tarsus of Cilicia, a center of learning.
- Learned the trade of tent making (Acts 18:3).
- A Jew from the tribe of Benjamin, educated under Rabbi Gamaliel (Acts 22:3).
- He exceeded his contemporaries in religious zeal (Galatians 1:14).
- As a young Pharisee, he watched Stephen being stoned to death (Acts 7:58; 8:1).

TIME LINE OF PAUL'S LIFE		
Date (A.D.)	Event	Bible reference
5	Birth of Saul	See Acts 7:58 "young man"; Philemon 9 "old man"
35	Martyrdom of Stephen	Acts 7:57–60. The witnesses laid their clothes at Saul's feet
35	Conversion	Recorded three times: Acts 9:1–19; 22:4–16; 26:9–18
35–8	Time in Arabia	Galatians 1:17. "I went immediately into Arabia"
38	Two week visit to Jerusalem	Acts 9:26–29; Galatians 1:18–19
38–43	Work in Cilicia and Syria	Acts 9:30; Galatians 1:21
43–44	Famine visit	Acts 11:27–30; 12:25
46–48	First missionary journey	Acts 13:2–14:28
49–50	Jerusalem conference	Acts 15:1–29
51–52	Appears before Gallio	Acts 18:12–17
50–52	Second missionary journey	Acts 15:40–18:23
52	Returns to Jerusalem	Acts 18:22
53–57	Third missionary journey	Acts 18:23–21:17
53–55	Visits Ephesus	Acts 19:1–20:1
57	Arrest in Jerusalem	Acts 21:27–22:30
57–59	Imprisoned in Caesarea	Acts 23:23–26:32
59	Voyage to Rome: shipwreck	Acts 27:1–28:16
59–61	First imprisonment in Rome	Acts 28:16–31
62–67	Fourth missionary journey	This included work in Crete, Titus 1:5
67–68	Second imprisonment in Rome	2 Timothy 4:6–8
67–68	Martyrdom	

POSSIBLE ORDER OF LETTERS WRITTEN BY PAUL

Date (A.D.)	Name of letter	Written from
51	1 Thessalonians	Corinth
51–52	2 Thessalonians	Corinth
51–52	Galatians	Corinth
55	1 Corinthians	Ephesus
55	2 Corinthians	Macedonia
57	Romans	Corinth or Cenchrea
60	Ephesians	Rome
60	Colossians	Rome
60	Philemon	Rome
61	Philippians	Rome
63–65	1 Timothy	Philippi
63–65	Titus	Philippi
67–68	2 Timothy	Mamertime prison

- Before his conversion, he cruelly persecuted Christians.
- He encountered the risen Christ in his conversion on the road to Damascus (Acts 9:1–19).
- After spending three years in Arabia, Barnabas introduced him to the apostles in Jerusalem.
- A plot against his life forced him to leave Jerusalem after fifteen days (Acts 9:26–30; Galatians 1:18–21).

Theological summary of Paul's conversion: Acts 9:1–22

1. He was converted from being an enemy of Jesus (1–2).
2. He was convicted by Jesus (3–4).
3. He was called by Jesus (5).
4. He surrendered to Jesus (6).
5. He prayed to Jesus (11).
6. He was baptized (18).
7. He witnessed for Jesus (20–22).

The persecuted apostle Paul

Being a follower of Jesus in the first century often involved being persecuted. Paul's life is one long list of harassment, trials, abuse, hounding, and persecution, most probably ending up with his martyrdom in Rome in

A.D. 67–68 under the exceedingly cruel Emperor Nero. He was:

- frequently imprisoned
- flogged severely
- stoned
- shipwrecked
- exposed to death again and again
- constantly on the move
- in danger from bandits
- often without sleep because of his labors
- often without food
- forced to escape like a fugitive from Damascus, being lowered over the wall in a basket
- thought of as the scum of the earth
- treated as if he was the refuse of the world

(1 Corinthians 4:10–13; 2 Corinthians 11:23–28).

Paul was constantly persecuted for his faith and martyred in Rome.

Against the background of Paul's persecution and suffering, verses such as this were written:

"For Christ's sake, I delight in weaknesses, in insults, in hardships, in persecutions, in difficulties. For when I am weak, then I am strong."

2 Corinthians 12:10

New Testament People

After each name its meaning appears, which in most cases is highly significant. A short description of each person then follows, ending with relevant Bible references for further information about the person.

People closely linked to Jesus

- Mary (*loved by God*). She became the mother of Jesus, probably in her mid-teens.
  Luke 1–2
- Joseph (*increaser*). Joseph, Jesus' foster father, obeyed God in his dreams.
  Matthew 1–2
- John the Baptist (*the Lord is gracious*). Baptized Jesus; was beheaded.
  Matthew 3; 11; 14
- Jesus (*the Lord is salvation*). He died for the sins of his people.
  Matthew, Mark, Luke, John
- Anna (*grace*). A faithful elderly prophetess. Met the baby Jesus in the temple.
  Luke 2:36–38
- King Herod (*heroic*). Evil king of Judah who tried to murder the toddler Jesus.
  Matthew 2
- Simeon (*he hears*). The Nunc dimittis are his words of praise as he met Jesus.
  Luke 2:25–35

The apostle Peter's name means "rock."

The twelve apostles

- Peter (*rock*). The leading apostle. Became a fearless Christian preacher.
  Matthew 4; 14; 16; 26
- Andrew (*manly*). Brother of Peter and fishing partner with James and John.
  Matthew 4:18–20
- James (*Greek form of Jacob*). With Peter and John, one of the inner three.
  Matthew 4:21–22
- John (*the Lord is gracious*). The "beloved disciple" who cared for Mary.
  John 19:25–27
- Philip (*lover of horses*). Fisherman who brought Bartholomew to Jesus.
  John 1:43–51
- Bartholomew (*son of Talmai*). Only mentioned in the lists of apostles.
  Matthew 10:3
- Thomas (*twin*). "Doubting," as he did not believe in Jesus' resurrection.
  John 20:24–28
- Matthew (*gift of the Lord*). Tax collector who left everything to follow Jesus.
  Matthew 9–10
- James (*Jacob*). Called "son of Alphaeus" to distinguish him from other James.
  Matthew 10:3
- Judas (*praise*). Had the surname "Thaddaeus" to distinguish him from Judas Iscariot.
  Luke 6:16
- Simon (*hearing*). Called "the Zealot" as he was probably a revolutionary.
  Matthew 10:4
- Judas (*praise*) Iscariot. He betrayed Jesus and hanged himself.
  Matthew 26:1–27:10

People who met Jesus

- Nicodemus (*conqueror of the people*). Pharisee who became a Christian.
  John 3; 7; 19
- Mary (*form of Miriam, meaning strong*). First to see risen Jesus.
  John 19:25; 20:1–18

- Lazarus (*God has helped*). After being dead for four days, he was raised by Jesus.
  John 11:1–12:11
- Martha (*lady*). Complained that her sister Mary sat and listened to Jesus.
  Luke 10:38–42
- Mary (*form of Miriam*). Sister of Martha and Lazarus, friend of Jesus.
  Mark 14:3–9
- Zacchaeus (*pure*). Chief tax collector who became a Christian.
  Luke 19
- Jairus (*he will enlighten*). Jesus healed his twelve-year-old daughter.
  Mark 5:21–43
- Pilate (*javelin carrier*). Roman governor who sentenced Jesus to death.
  John 18:28–19:22
- Simon (*he hears*). Simon of Cyrene carried Jesus' cross for him.
  Matthew 27:32
- Joseph (*may [God] add*) of Arimathea. Put body of Jesus in his new tomb.
  John 19:38–42

Some of the first Christians

- Stephen (*crown*). First Christian martyr.
  Acts 6:1–8:2
- Cleopas (*renowned father*). Walked on road to Emmaus with risen Jesus.
  Luke 24:13–49
- Cornelius (*of a horn*). Roman centurion converted to Christ through Peter.
  Acts 10
- Matthias (*gift of God*). Chosen as a replacement apostle for Judas Iscariot.
  Acts 1:15–26
- Agabus (*locust*). Jerusalem prophet who prophesied a famine.
  Acts 11:27–30; 21:10–11
- Philip (*lover of horses*). Evangelist who explained the gospel to Ethiopian.
  Acts 8:26–39
- Dorcas (*gazelle*). Helper of poor, brought back to life by Peter.
  Acts 9:36–43

Paul's helpers and friends

Priscilla offered her house as a meeting place for Christians.

- Paul (*small*). Apostle and pioneering missionary.
  Acts 7; 9–28; Paul's letters
- Silas (*wood-dweller*). Companion of Paul.
  Acts 15–18
- Titus (*honored*). Companion of Paul. Worked in Crete.
  Titus
- Barnabas (*son of encouragement*). Introduced Paul to Jerusalem church.
  Acts 4, 9, 11
- Timothy (*honoring God*). Young church leader, greatly helped by Paul.
  1 and 2 Timothy
- Luke (*light-giving*). Historian, doctor, traveling companion of Paul.
  Luke and Acts
- Priscilla (*ancient one*). House-churches met in her homes in Ephesus and Rome.
  Acts 18
- Apollos (*a destroyer*). Christian from Alexandria who taught Christians.
  Acts 18:24–19:1
- Demas (*popular*). Deserted Paul while a prisoner in Rome.
  Colossians 4:14; 2 Timothy 4:10
- Onesimus (*profitable*). Runaway slave. Converted through Paul in prison in Rome.
  Philemon
- Philemon (*friendship*). Asked by Paul to receive back Onesimus.
  Philemon
- Epaphroditus (*handsome*). "Put his life in danger" to help Paul.
  Philippians 2:19–30; 4:18
- Eutychus (*fortunate*). Fell out of window while listening to Paul preaching.
  Acts 20:7–12
- Lydia (*native of Lydia*). Business woman converted through Paul's preaching.
  Acts 16:1–15

4

Introducing Bible Teaching

82–83
Teaching about God the Father

84–85
Teaching about the Holy Spirit

86–87
The Parables of Jesus

88–89
Symbolic Language

90–91
Prayer

92–93
Humankind

94–95
What Jesus Taught

96–97
Salvation and the Cross of Jesus

98–99
The Love of God

100–101
Satan Unmasked

102–103
The End of the World

Teaching about God the Father

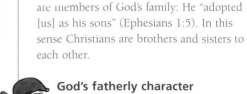

GOD AS FATHER

God the Father is seen as the Creator God

- God is spoken of as Father of the Jews: "Is he not your Father, your Creator, who made you and formed you?" (Deuteronomy 32:6).
- Malachi reminds unfaithful Judah: "Have we not all one Father? Did not one God create us?" (Malachi 2:10).
- Isaiah pleads with God not to forsake his people: "Yet, O LORD, you are our Father. We are the clay, you are the potter; we are all the work of your hand" (Isaiah 64:8).
- Jesus sometimes used the title Father for God to emphasize his providential care of wild life: "Look at the birds of the air . . . your heavenly Father feeds them" (Matthew 6:26). Jesus also emphasizes God's providential care of humans (Matthew 5:45; 10:30).

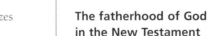

You are our Father. We are the clay, you are the potter; we are all the work of your hand.

Is God Father to everyone?

Since God created everyone, we can all claim that we were made in the image of God, and to have been made by the Creator God. But, in Jesus' teaching, the Fatherhood of God is restricted to believers only. Jesus said to some unbelieving Jews, "You belong to your father, the devil" (John 8:44).

God is Father of us all.

God is the spiritual Father of those who are members of God's family: He "adopted [us] as his sons" (Ephesians 1:5). In this sense Christians are brothers and sisters to each other.

God's fatherly character in the Old Testament
The idea of the fatherhood of God was evident in the Old Testament.

- "In the desert . . . you saw how the LORD your God carried you, as a father carries his son" (Deuteronomy 1:31).
- "As a father has compassion on his children, so the LORD has compassion on those who fear him" (Psalm 103:13).
- "A father to the fatherless, a defender of widows, is God in his holy dwelling" (Psalm 68:5).

The fatherhood of God in the New Testament
The fatherhood of God is seen most clearly in the teaching of Jesus. There is no other concept of God which is stressed more strongly in the New Testament than the fatherhood of God.

Jesus taught his disciples, "Your heavenly Father knows" (Matthew 6:32) about their everyday needs.

The title Father is used for God at the start of every letter of the apostle Paul. "Grace and peace to you from God our Father" (Ephesians 1:2).

The title Father is sometimes qualified, giving added richness to it

- God is often described as "the God and Father of our Lord Jesus Christ" (Ephesians 1:3).
- "the glorious Father" (Ephesians 1:17).
- "We [should] submit to the Father of our spirits and live" (Hebrews 12:9).

- "Every good and perfect gift is from above, coming down from the Father of the heavenly lights, who does not change like shifting shadows" (James 1:17).

God has motherly as well as fatherly characteristics.

- Human fatherhood is derived from the fatherhood of God: "I kneel before the Father, from whom his whole family in heaven and on earth derives its name" (Ephesians 3:14–15).

Abba

In the garden of Gethsemane, Jesus prayed to his heavenly Father using the word *Abba*. This was originally an Aramaic way of speaking to a father. It was used by young children, the equivalent to saying Daddy or Dad today. When Jesus used this word, which was never used in the Old Testament, it showed that his view of God as Father excluded any ideas of a formal approach to him:

- "*Abba*, Father, . . . everything is possible for you. Take this cup from me" (Mark 14:36).
- Jesus' followers were to address God the Father in this new and intimate way as well: "You received the Spirit of sonship. And by him we cry, '*Abba*, Father'" (Romans 8:15).
- "Because you are sons, God sent the Spirit of his Son into our hearts, the Spirit who calls out, '*Abba*, Father'" (Galatians 4:6).

The motherly characteristics of God

The Bible's teaching about God embraces the concept of the "motherhood" of God as well as the "fatherhood" of God. It finds no contradiction in saying in some places that God is like a father and in other places that God can be likened to a mother.

God is likened to a comforting mother: "You will . . . be carried on her arm and dandled on her knees. As a mother comforts her child, so will I comfort you" (Isaiah 66:12–13).

THREE IN ONE

The Trinity

The word Trinity does not appear in the Bible. The word *Trinitas* was first used in the A.D. 190s and later was officially incorporated into the teaching of the Christian church. The doctrine of the Trinity affirms three things:

- There is only one God.
- The Father, and the Son, and the Holy Spirit are each God.
- The Father, and the Son, and the Holy Spirit are each a distinct Person.

Father, Son, and Holy Spirit linked in Scripture

- "Jesus answered: . . . 'I will ask the Father, and he will give you another Counselor to be with you forever—the Spirit of truth'" (John 14:9, 16–17).
- "Jesus came to them and said, . . . 'Therefore go and make disciples of all nations, baptizing them in the name of the Father and of the Son and of the Holy Spirit'" (Matthew 28:18–19).
- "May the grace of the Lord Jesus Christ, and the love of God, and the fellowship of the Holy Spirit be with you all" (2 Corinthians 13:14).

Teaching about the Holy Spirit

The Holy Spirit is sometimes called the third Person of the Trinity. One way to appreciate who he is, is to look at what the Bible credits him as doing in the world and through people.

The Holy Spirit in action

He shares in creation. He inspires people to:

- build
- make beautiful things
- speak
- preach
- laugh
- sing
- make music.

He gives:

- courage
- leadership
- visions
- divine revelation
- dreams
- understanding about Jesus' death
- true reverence for God.

He helps people to:
- pray
- repent
- become humble
- yield stubborn wills.

The Holy Spirit can inspire laughter.

GIFTS OF THE HOLY SPIRIT IN THE NEW TESTAMENT

Gifts used for ministry of the word	Gifts used for ministry in deeds	Bible reference
Prophesying Teaching	Serving Encouraging Contributing to the needs of others Leadership Showing mercy	Romans 12:6–8
Wisdom Knowledge Prophecy Discernment Speaking in tongues Interpretation of tongues	Faith Healing Miracles Helping Gifts of administration	1 Corinthians 12:4–11, 28–30
Apostolic work Prophetic work Evangelistic work Pastoral work Teaching work		Ephesians 4:7–12

The purpose of the gifts

"To prepare God's people for works of service, so that the body of Christ may be built up until we all reach unity in the faith and in the knowledge of the Son of God and become mature, attaining to the whole measure of the fulness of Christ" (Ephesians 4:12–13).

The Holy Spirit in the Old Testament

The Holy Spirit was active from the beginning and his inspirational activity is recorded many times in the Old Testament.

The fruit of the Holy Spirit

"The fruit of the Spirit is love, joy, peace, patience, kindness, goodness, faithfulness, gentleness and self-control" (Galatians 5:22–23).

The gifts of the Holy Spirit

"We have different gifts, according to the grace given us" (Romans 12:5).

The Holy Spirit is often represented in the Bible and in many paintings by a dove, as at Jesus' Baptism.

For Christians, the dove symbolizes peace and hope, which are also provided by the Holy Spirit.

NO CHRISTIAN IS EXCLUDED

"Now you are the body of Christ, and each one of you is a part of it. And in the church God has appointed first of all apostles, second prophets, third teachers, then workers of miracles, also those who have gifts of healing, those able to help others, those with gifts of administration, and those speaking in different kinds of tongues. Are all apostles? Are all prophets? Are all teachers? Do all work miracles? Do all have gifts of healing? Do all speak in tongues? Do all interpret? But eagerly desire the greater gifts."

1 Corinthians 12:27–30

THE HOLY SPIRIT IN THE OLD TESTAMENT		
Occasion/person	Quote	Bible reference
Creation	The Spirit of God was hovering over the waters.	Genesis 1:2
The Tent of Meeting	I have chosen Bezalel . . . and I have filled him with the Spirit of God, with skill, ability and knowledge in all kinds of crafts.	Exodus 31:2–3
In the desert	The Spirit rested on [Eldad and Medad], and they prophesied in the camp.	Numbers 11:26
Joshua	Take Joshua . . . a man in whom is the spirit.	Numbers 27:18
Othniel	The Spirit of the Lord came upon . . . Othniel.	Judges 3:10
Gideon	The Spirit of the Lord came upon Gideon.	Judges 6:34
David's last words	The Spirit of the Lord spoke through me; his word was on my tongue.	2 Samuel 23:2
Isaiah's prophecy	. . . till the Spirit is poured upon us from on high.	Isaiah 32:15
Joel's prophecy	And afterwards, I will pour out my Spirit on all people. Your sons and daughters will prophesy, your old men will dream dreams, and your young men will see visions. Even on my servants, both men and women, I will pour out my Spirit in those days.	Joel 2:28–29

The Parables of Jesus

THE MEANING OF "PARABLE"

The word parable, from the Greek verb *paraballo*, means to lay one thing alongside another, and so to compare one thing with another thing.

JESUS AND PARABLES

The countryside and farming provided the basis for many parables.

The parables are the biggest single feature in all of Jesus' teaching: "[Jesus] did not say anything to them without using a parable" (Matthew 13:34).

Through his parables, Jesus used ordinary things to communicate spiritual realities.

The lost coin
Jesus' parable about the lost coin (Luke 15:8–10) shows that it is sometimes helpful to know about the customs of the first century in order to fully appreciate the impact of the story.

The woman in the story felt so terribly upset because in those days a woman often wore her dowry of coins on a string, like a necklace, but on the forehead, as part of her headdress. The dowry was of crucial importance to a woman. Its loss meant more than merely losing a dollar bill or a silver coin. The dowry given to a woman by her father often took the form of coins with holes drilled through them so that they could be strung together.

No parables in John's gospel
There are no parables as such in John's gospel.

John uses ordinary things to point to spiritual truths:
- Water (4:5–14)
- Harvest time (4:35–38)
- Bread (6:25–35)
- Water (7:37–39)
- Light (8:12)
- Shepherd (10:1–18)
- Grain of wheat (12:20–26)
- The vine (15:1–17).

Ordinary everyday things like water are used by John to point to spiritual truths.

THE PARABLES OF JESUS

Classification	Name of parable	Matthew	Mark	Luke
From everyday items in Bible times				
Light	Lamp under a bowl	5:14–15	4:21–22	8:16; 11:33
Building a house	Wise and foolish builders	7:24–27		6:47–49
Patching clothes	New cloth on old coat	9:16	2:21	5:36
New wine	New wine and old wineskins	9:17	2:22	5:37–38
Yeast	Yeast	13:33		13:20–21
Burying treasure	Hidden treasure	13:44		
Pearls	Pearl	13:45–46		
Fishing net	Net	13:47–50		
Servants	Faithful and wise servants	24:45–51		12:42–48
Lost coin	Lost coin			15:8–10
From farming and nature				
Farmer	The sower	13:3–8, 18–23	4:3–8, 14–20	8:5–8, 11–15
Weeds	Weeds	13:24–30, 36–43		
Mustard seed	Mustard seed	13:31–32	4:30–32	13:18–19
Lost sheep	Lost sheep	18:12–14		15:4–7
Vineyard	Workers in the vineyard	20:1–16		
Vineyard	Tenants	21:33–44	12:1–11	20:9–18
Sheep with goats	Sheep and goats	25:31–46		
Growing seed	Growing seed		4:26–29	
Unfruitful fig tree	Unfruitful fig tree			13:6–9
Fig tree	Fig tree	24:32–35	13:28–29	21:29–31
From everyday life				
New and old truths	Owner of a house	13:52		
Forgiveness	Unmerciful servant	18:23–34		
Two sons	Two sons	21:28–32		
Wedding party	Wedding banquet	22:2–14		14:15–24
Girls at a wedding	Ten virgins	25:1–13		
Servants	Talents	25:14–30		19:12–27
Watchful servants	Watchful servants		13:35–37	12:35–40
Debts and debtors	Money-lender			7:41–43
Mugging	Good Samaritan			10:30–37
Friend in need	Friend in need			11:5–8
Rich fool	Rich fool			12:16–21
Humility and hospitality	Lowest seat at the feast			14:7–14
Counting the cost	Cost of being a disciple			14:28–33
Lost son	Lost son			15:11–32
Shrewd manager	Shrewd manager			16:1–8
Rich man, beggar	Rich man and Lazarus			16:19–31
Persistent widow	Persistent widow			18:2–8
Pharisee and tax collector	Pharisee and tax collector			18:10–14

A lamp, when lit, should not be hidden.

Symbolic Language

Many words and numbers used in the Bible have symbolic meanings and theological significance.

Catacombs of Rome

To escape persecution from Roman soldiers, early Christians sought refuge in the catacombs (underground burial places) where the soldiers would not enter because they were superstitious. Paintings and inscriptions, such as the sign of the anchor and the sign of the fish (*ichthus*), dating back to A.D. 72, have been discovered there. The Greek letter "X" was used as one of these earliest inscriptions. X symbolized Christ, as X in Greek is "Chi," the first letter in the name of Christ.

Ichthus

The symbol of the fish became a secret sign of the early Christians. The Greek word for "fish" is *ichthus*. It stood for:

> I: *Iesous*—Jesus (I in Greek is J in English)
> Ch: *Christos*—Christ
> Th: *Theou*—God's
> U: *Uios*—Son
> S: *Soter*—Savior.

WORDS WITH SYMBOLIC MEANING

Word	Example	Meaning	Bible reference
Abomination	Their souls delight in their abominations.	Sin in general	Isaiah 66:3; Ezekiel 16:50–51
Adultery	Those who commit adultery with her.	Backsliding	Revelation 2:22
Anchor	We have this hope as an anchor for the soul.	Security	Hebrews 6:19
Anoint	God anointed Jesus of Nazareth with the Holy Spirit and power.	Confer power	Acts 10:38
Ashes	I repent in dust and ashes.	Humiliation	Job 42:6
Book of life	I will never blot out his name from the book of life.	Heavenly register of God's people	Revelation 3:5
Bride	The bride, the wife of the Lamb	The church	Revelation 21:9
Chaff	They are like chaff.	Non religious people	Psalm 1:4
Face	Let your face shine on your servant.	God's favor	Psalm 31:16
Harlot	See how the faithful city has become a harlot.	Apostasy	Isaiah 1:21; Revelation 17:5
High places	He rebuilt the high places.	Idolatrous altars	2 Kings 21:1–9
Horn	Moab's horn is cut off.	Power	Jeremiah 48:25
Legs	Nor his delight in the legs of a man.	Natural strength	Psalm 147:10
Linen	Fine linen, bright and clean, was given her to wear.	Righteousness	Leviticus 16:23 Revelation 19:8
Naked	We will not be found naked.	Lacking God's righteousness	2 Corinthians 5:3; Revelation 3:17
Sackcloth	Fasting and wearing sackcloth.	Humility	Nehemiah 9:1
Sun	For the Lord is a sun.	God's grace	Psalm 84:11
Temple	You yourselves are God's temple.	Believer's body	1 Corinthians 3:16–17; 6:19–20

THE MEANINGS OF HAND EXPRESSIONS

Movement of hand	Meaning	Bible reference
To be at the right hand of	To have authority	Mark 14:62
Hollow of the hand	Place of security	Isaiah 40:12
Hand of the Lord on	To prophecy	Ezekiel 37:1
To lay hands on	To bless or ordain	1 Timothy 5:22
To lift hands	To pray, bless, ask for help	Psalm 28:2
To wash hands	To show innocence A ritual for cleansing	Matthew 27:24 Mark 7:4
To put a hand under a thigh	To take a solemn oath	Genesis 47:29

144,000

Revelation 7:4 and 14:1 record 144,000 "who were sealed."

The number 144,000 has been broken down in the following way.

12 stands for the number of election: the 12 tribes of Israel, the 12 apostles. So the number 12 is squared (multiplied by itself).

1,000 represents an infinitely large number, symbolizing the complete number of saints of both covenants who are preserved by God.

12 x 12 x 1,000 = 144,000.

The number 12, as in the number of tribes of Israel, had theological significance.

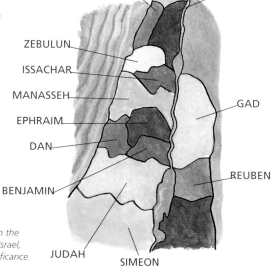

NUMBERS WITH SYMBOLIC MEANING

Occasion/person	Quote	Bible reference
1	Unity	John 17:21–23; Deuteronomy 6:4
3	Trinity	Matthew 28:19; John 14:26;15:26; 2 Corinthians 13:14; 1 Peter 1:2
6	Man	Genesis 1:17; Revelation 13:18
7	Completion, fulfillment, perfection	Leviticus 16:29; 4:6; 2 Kings 5:10; Exodus 25:32
12	God's purposes	Genesis 49:28; Matthew 10:1ff
40	New era of God's mighty acts	Genesis 7:17; 8:6; Exodus 24:18; 34:28; Deuteronomy 9:9; Jonah 3:4
70	Carrying out God's work	Genesis 46:27; Numbers 11:16; Jeremiah 25:11; 29:10; Luke 10:1
666	Number of the beast	Revelation 13:18
1000	Limitless time or number	Psalm 90:4, 2 Peter 3:8; Daniel 7:10; Revelation 5:11

Prayer

The Psalms, the hymn book of the Jews, contain a large number of prayers that are used by Christians for singing in public and meditating in private.

PRAYERS RECORDED IN THE BIBLE

Many of God's outstanding men and women of faith have their prayers recorded in the Bible.

Phylacteries and prayer

From about the second century B.C., all male Jews were expected to wear two phylacteries (tephillim).

PRAYERS IN THE PSALMS

Topic	Psalm
Evening prayer	4
Morning prayer	5
Shepherd prayer	23
Worship and praise	24; 67; 92; 95–98; 100; 113; 145; 148; 150
God's word	19; 119
Guidance	25
God's protection	46; 91; 125
Trust	37; 62
God's glory	8; 29; 93; 104
Deliverance	40; 116
God's love and care	89; 103; 107; 146
Longing for God	27; 42; 63; 84
Help in trouble	66; 69; 86; 88; 102; 140; 143
Thanksgiving	65; 111; 136
Forgiveness	51; 130

TEN WAYS TO PRAY

- Do not cherish sin in your heart
  Psalm 66:18
- Be trusting in God
  Psalm 37:5
- Do not doubt
  James 1:6
- In the name of Jesus
  John 14:13
- With a forgiving spirit
  Mark 11:25–26
- In obedience
  John 3.22
- In genuine repentance
  Luke 18:13–14
- In line with God's law
  Proverbs 28:9
- From a godly heart
  Psalm 32:6

- The phylacteries were small boxes about an inch and a half (38 mm) square.
- They were made of leather from ritually clean animals.
- One was fastened on the forehead.
- One was wound round the left forearm by a leather thong.
- They had to be worn at morning prayers.
- The boxes contained tiny rolled-up scrolls of scripture.
- The four passages were Exodus 13:1–10, 11–16; Deuteronomy 6:4–9; 11:3–21.

Mezuzot

Mezuzot (singular mezuzah) were small wooden or metal containers in which passages of Scripture were placed. Mezuzot were attached to the door frames of Jewish houses, and sometimes worn round the neck.

TWENTY OLD TESTAMENT PRAYERS

Bible person	Event	Bible reference
1. Abraham	Prays for Sodom	Genesis 18:22–23
2. Abraham's servant	Prays for guidance	Genesis 24:12–14
3. Isaac	Blesses Jacob	Genesis 27
4. Jacob	Prays at Penuel	Genesis 32
5. Moses	Song of thanks for deliverance	Exodus 15
6. Moses	Blesses Israelites	Deuteronomy 33
7. Joshua	Prays for victory	Joshua 10
8. Deborah	Song of thanks for victory	Judges 5
9. Gideon	Prays for signs	Judges 6
10. Hannah	Prays for a son	1 Samuel 1
11. Samuel	Prays for the nation	1 Samuel 7
12. David	Prayer of repentance	Psalm 51
13. Solomon	Prays for wisdom	1 Kings 3
14. Solomon	Dedicating the temple	1 Kings 8
15. Elijah	Prays on Mount Carmel	1 Kings 18
16. Nehemiah	Prays for his people	Nehemiah 1
17. Job	Confesses his wrong	Job 42
18. Hezekiah	Prays in his illness	Isaiah 38
19. Jeremiah	Complains and praises God	Jeremiah 20
20. Jonah	From inside the great fish	Jonah 2

SHEMA

"Hear, O Israel: The LORD our God, the
LORD is one. Love the LORD your God
with all your heart and with all your soul
and with all your strength. These
commandments that I give you today are
to be upon your hearts. Impress them on
your children. Talk about them when you
sit at home and when you walk along the
road, when you lie down and when you
get up. Tie them as symbols on your
hands and bind them on your foreheads.
Write them on the door frames of your
houses and on your gates."

෴ *Deuteronomy 6:4–9*

These verses from Deuteronomy 6:4–9,
known as the *Shema*, from the Hebrew "Hear,"
were recited daily by the pious Jews and
became a confession of faith for them.

See also: *Jesus and Prayer*, pp. 42–43.

A PSALM OF PRAISE AND WORSHIP

"May God be gracious to us and bless us
and make his face shine upon us, that your
ways may be known on earth, your
salvation among all nations. May the
peoples praise you, O God; may all the
peoples praise you. May the nations be
glad and sing for joy, for you rule the
peoples justly and guide the nations of the
earth. May the peoples praise you, O God;
may all the peoples praise you. Then the
land will yield its harvest, and God, our
God, will bless us. God will bless us, and
all the ends of the earth will fear him."

෴ *Psalm 67*

*Prayer can
take place
anywhere,
in public
or private*

Humankind

All men and women, no matter how pious, are between angels and animals in the created order.

THE HUMAN RACE

What the Bible teaches us about the human race

• **Its origin—divine**
Adam and Eve were created by a direct creative act of God (Genesis 1–2).

• **Its identity—in God's image**
Humans were created in the image of God. (Genesis 1:26).

Humans are alienated from God because of the Fall.

• **Its position— between angels and animals**
Humankind, in God's created order, is between angels and animals: "God . . . said . . . 'Rule over the fish of the sea and the birds of the air and over every living creature that moves on the ground'" (Genesis 1:28).

• **Its fall—corrupted by sin**
Because of the Fall, the act of sin deliberately indulged in by Adam and Eve (Genesis 3), humankind is alienated from God.

New creation
It is true that humankind retains God's image, no matter how corrupt it becomes. But, because of the Fall, humankind is in need of a "new creation" (2 Corinthians 5:17).

A division
Humankind can be divided thus:
• In Christ and not in Christ
• Born again and not born again
• Forgiven and unforgiven.

SINNERS AND SAINTS	
SINNERS	**SAINTS**
Children of wrath (Ephesians 2:3)	Children of God (Romans 8:16–17)
Dead in sin (Ephesians 2:1)	Alive with Christ (Ephesians 2:5)
Taught by Satan (2 Corinthians 11;13–15)	Taught by God (1 John 2:27)
Follower of the ways of the world (Ephesians 2:2)	Walks in the light (Ephesians 5:8)
Cursed (Galatians 3:10)	Redeemed from the curse (Galatians 3:13)
Far from God (Ephesians 2:13)	Brought near to God (Ephesians 2:13)
Without God (Ephesians 2:12)	With God (1 John 4:15–9)
Under God's wrath (John 3:36)	Saved from God's wrath (Romans 5:9)
Without Christ (Ephesians 2:12)	Christ in you (Colossians 1:17)

WHAT IS MAN?

". . . what is man that you are
mindful of him, the son of man
that you care for him? You made
him a little lower than the
heavenly beings and crowned him
with glory and honor. You made
him ruler over the works of your
hands; you put everything under
his feet: all flocks and herds, and
the beasts of the field, the birds of
the air, and the fish of the sea, all
that swim the paths of the sea."

Psalm 8:4–8

SINNERS AND SAINTS

The Bible constantly emphasizes the
difference between the saved and the
unsaved. One way to appreciate this is to
reflect on the characteristics that are given
to saints and sinners.

Sinners

One of the clearest verses to describe a sinner
is Romans 3:23. It shows that the basic evil of
sin is falling short of God's standards and his

SINNERS AND SAINTS COMPARED (EPHESIANS 2:1–6)

Sinners

"As for you, you were dead in your transgressions
and sins, in which you used to live when you
followed the ways of this world and of the ruler
of the kingdom of the air, the spirit who is now at
work in those who are disobedient. All of us also
lived among them at one time, gratifying the
cravings of our own sinful nature and following
its desires and thoughts. Like the rest, we were by
nature children of wrath . . . even when we were
dead in transgressions."

Saints

"But because of his great love for us, God, who
is rich in mercy made us alive with Christ—it is
by grace you have been saved. And God raised
us up with Christ and seated us with him in the
heavenly realms in Christ Jesus."

glory. This chapter of Paul's letter clearly
warns believers about the dangers of sin.

Saints

In the New Testament "saint" is a synonym for
a Christian. When Paul in Ephesians 1:15
writes about "your love for all the saints," he is
saying "your love for all your fellow Christians."

And Paul described himself humbly as
being less than the least of the saints
(Ephesians 3:8).

*God created humankind to rule
over animals, birds, and fish.*

What Jesus Taught

THE SERMON ON THE MOUNT

In Matthew 5–7 Jesus' longest set of teachings is recorded. It includes three types of material:
- Beatitudes: declarations of blessedness (5:1–12)
- ethical instructions (5:13–20; 6:1–7:23)
- contrasts between Jesus' ethical teaching and Jewish teaching (5:21–48).

ANALYSIS OF THE SERMON ON THE MOUNT

The subjects of the kingdom	**5:1–16**
The Beatitudes	5:1–12
The witnesses (salt and light)	5:13–16
Jesus' relationship to the law	**5:17–7:6**
Jesus fulfills the law	5:17–19
Jesus rejects the Pharisees' interpretation	5:20–48
Murder	5:20–26
Adultery	5:27–30
Divorce	5:31–32
Oaths	5:33–37
Retaliation	5:38–42
Love for enemies	5:43–48
Jesus rejects the practices of the Pharisees	6:1–7:6
Giving to the needy	6:1–4
Prayer	6:5–15
Fasting	6:16–18
Wealth	6:19–34
Judging	7:1–6
Jesus' instructions about entering the kingdom	**7:7–27**
"Ask, seek, knock"	7:7–27
The Golden Rule	7:12
Two ways of life	7:13–14
False and true teaching	7:15–20
The true way into the kingdom	7:21–23
The two builders	7:24–27

The best-known parts of the Sermon on the Mount

The Sermon on the Mount only takes fifteen minutes to read through, but it is probably the most influential of all the teachings of Jesus:
- The Beatitudes (5:3–12)
- "Love your enemies" (5:43–48)
- The Lord's Prayer (6:9–13)
- "Do not worry" (6:25–34)
- "Ask, seek, knock" (7:7–12)
- The wise and foolish builders (7:24–27).

Blessed are those who hunger and thirst for righteousness, for they will be filled.

Jesus' teaching

Jesus taught about many different topics and nearly the complete record of this comes in the gospels of Matthew, Mark, Luke, and John.

THE BEATITUDES

"Blessed are the poor in spirit, for theirs is the kingdom of heaven. Blessed are those who mourn, for they will be comforted. Blessed are the meek, for they will inherit the earth. Blessed are those who hunger and thirst for righteousness, for they will be filled. Blessed are the merciful, for they will be shown mercy. Blessed are the pure in heart, for they will see God. Blessed are the peacemakers, for they will be called sons of God. Blessed are those who are persecuted because of righteousness, for theirs is the kingdom of heaven. Blessed are you when people insult you, persecute you and falsely say all kinds of evil against you because of me. Rejoice and be glad, because great is your reward in heaven, for in the same way they persecuted the prophets who were before you."

Matthew 5:3–12

JESUS' TEACHING SUMMARIZED BY SUBJECT

Topic	Matthew	Mark	Luke	John
Anger	5:21–26			
Discipleship	10:34–39; 16:24–28	1:14–20	9:21–27; 57–62; 14:25–33 10:1–12;	14–17
Divorce and remarriage	5:31–32;	19:1–12	16:18	
Eternal life	19:16–30		10:25–37; 18:18–30	3:1–21; 4:1–41; 5:19–47; 10:7–30; 12:44–50
Faith	18:6–9; 21:18–22	11:20–25	17:5–6	
Fasting	6:16–18	9:14–17	2:18–22	5:33–39
Forgiveness and sin	18:21–35; 26:26–29	1:14–15	7:36–50; 17:1–4	8:1–11
God				3:1–21; 8:12–30
Happiness	5:3–12		6:20–26; 11:27–28	
Himself	16:13–21; 20:17–19; 26:26–35	8:31–38; 10:32–34	4:16–30; 9:21–27; 20:1–8	3:1–21; 10; 11:17–27; 14–17
Judgment	11:20–24; 12:33–42; 25:31–46			12:44–50
Judging others	7:1–5		6:37–42	
Kingdom of God	5–7; 13; 18:1–5; 19:13–30; 20–25	1:14–15	13:18–30; 18:18–30; 19:11–27; 22:24–30	3:1–21
Love	5:38–48		6:27–36; 10:25–37	13:20–35; 14–17
New birth				3:1–21
Obedience	7:24–27		8:11–18	14:15–15:17
Peace				14:27–31
Persecution	10:16–25			15:18–27
Prayer	6:5–15; 21:18–22	11:20–25	11:1–13; 18:1–8	
Resurrection	22:23–33	12:18–27	20:27–39	
Service	20:20–28	10:35–45		13:1–20
Taxes	22:15–22	12:13–17	20:19–26	
Trust	6:25–34		12:22–31	
Wealth and possessions	6:19–21, 24;		12:13–21; 12:32–34; 16:1–13; 18:18–30	
Worry	10:26–31		12:4–7	14:1–14
Worship				4:1–26

Salvation and the Cross of Jesus

SALVATION
AND THE CROSS

Our salvation is bound up with the cross of Jesus.

The Bible writers use the word salvation to refer to being saved from sin and forgiven and pardoned by God.

The Old Testament prefigures the cross of Jesus

God provided the Old Testament sacrifices as a way of salvation, and New Testament writers often talk about Jesus' "sacrifice."

Leviticus 1–7, a kind of handbook for sacrifice, describes five kinds of sacrifice:

- *Burnt offerings*
  The burning of the sacrifice symbolized Israel's desire to rid itself of its sinful acts against God (Leviticus 6:13).
- *Grain offerings*
  Leviticus 2 mentions four kinds of grain offerings, which had a similar purpose to burnt offerings.
- *Fellowship offerings*, or "peace" offerings
  This ritual meal was shared with God, the priests, and sometimes other worshipers. It depicted harmony between God and man (Leviticus 3:1–17).

Jesus' death on the cross was his sacrifice for us and the means to our salvation.

- *Sin offerings*
  These were to atone for our sinful nature. The sacrifices for sin "paid off" or expiated a worshiper's ritual faults against the Lord (Leviticus 4:1–5:13).
- *Guilt offerings*, or "trespass" offerings
  These were similar to sin offerings (Leviticus 5:14–6:7).

THE CROSS IN THE
NEW TESTAMENT

The cross of Jesus in the gospels

The buildup to and crucifixion of Jesus takes up more space in the gospels than any other event:

- Jesus was crucified at a place called Golgotha (Matthew 27:33; Mark 15:24).
- Jesus actually died: "He breathed his last" (Luke 23:46).
- Jesus explained the meaning of his death: "Did not the Christ have to suffer these things and then enter his glory?" (Luke 24:26).

"Father, forgive them, for they do not know what they are doing" (Luke 23:34).

Jesus answered [one of the two dying thieves], "I tell you the truth, today you will be with me in paradise" (Luke 23:43).

When Jesus saw his mother there, and the disciple whom he loved standing nearby, he said to his mother, "Dear woman, here is your son," and to the disciple, "Here is your mother." From that time on, this disciple took her into his home (John 19:26–27).

About the ninth hour Jesus cried out in a loud voice, "Eloi, Eloi, lama sabachthani?"—which means, "My God, my God, why have you forsaken me?" (Matthew 27:46).

"I am thirsty" (John 19:28).

"It is finished" (John 19:30).

"Father, into your hands I commit my spirit" (Luke 23:46).

- John the Baptist says of Jesus, "Look, the Lamb of God, who takes away the sin of the world!" (John 1:29).
- Jesus linked his death with his resurrection (John 12:32).
- Jesus was conscious that he was carrying out God the Father's plan through his death: "I have brought you glory on earth by completing the work you gave me to do" (John 17:4).

The cross of Jesus in the New Testament letters

The New Testament letter writers make the cross of Jesus their centerpiece as they explain God's plan of salvation:

- Paul spent his time writing and preaching about the cross of Jesus: "We preach Christ crucified" (1 Corinthians 1:23).
- Paul also frequently linked the Old Testament sacrifices with Jesus' personal sacrifice on the cross: "For Christ, our Passover lamb, has been sacrificed" (1 Corinthians 5:7).

- Jesus' sacrifice is a model for Christians: "Live a life of love, just as Christ loved us and gave himself up for us as a fragrant offering and sacrifice to God" (Ephesians 5:2).
- The cross of Jesus was central to everything Paul did: "May I never boast except in the cross of our Lord Jesus Christ, through which the world has been crucified to me, and I to the world" (Galatians 6:14).
- Peter refers to Jesus as a lamb. "You were redeemed . . . with the precious blood of Christ, a lamb without blemish or defect" (1 Peter 1:18–19).

Jesus' seven words from the cross

When Jesus died on the cross, the gospel writers record that he spoke or prayed seven times. These seven sentences are sometimes called "the seven words from the cross."

Jesus the Lamb
in the book of Revelation

Jesus is called the Lamb 29 times in the book of Revelation, stressing the sacrificial nature of his death.

Like the offering of a lamb, Jesus' death was a blood sacrifice.

Jesus as our substitute

The idea of Jesus dying in our place on the cross is inescapable in his teaching, and the concept is found throughout the New Testament "For . . . the Son of Man . . . came . . . to give his life as a ransom for many" (Mark 10:45).

The Love of God

DIFFERENT WORDS FOR LOVE

Three Greek words for love

- *Eros*. This was the Greek word for erotic love.
- *Philia*. This was the Greek word for friendship and love between equals, and it is found as part of many English words today.
- *Agape*. When the writers of the New Testament wanted to talk about God's love, a pure self-giving love that claimed no tinge of self-interest, they employed the little-used term in Classical Greek *agape*. When these writers wanted to refer to the love of God in Jesus, they used the word *agape*.

GOD'S LOVE IN THE OLD TESTAMENT

It is a false impression that God is a God of wrath in the Old Testament, but a God of love in the New Testament. Many of the outstanding images of God's love come from the Old Testament.

Although there are several instances of God showing his wrath, the Old Testament, as well as the New Testament, also portrays God as a God of love:

- "The LORD loved him [Solomon]; and because the LORD loved him, he sent word through Nathan the prophet to name him Jedidiah [loved by the LORD]" (2 Samuel 12:24).
- "The LORD is my shepherd" (Psalm 23:1).
- "[The LORD says,] 'I am the Lord, your God, the Holy One of Israel, your Savior; . . . I love you'" (Isaiah 43:3–4).
- "I will comfort you" (Isaiah 66:13).
- "I have loved you with an everlasting love; I have drawn you with loving-kindness" (Jeremiah 31:3).

GOD'S LOVE FOR ISRAEL

"When Israel was a child, I loved him,
and out of Egypt I called my son . . .
It was I who taught Ephraim to walk,
taking them by the arms; but they did
not realize it was I who healed them.
I led them with cords of human
kindness, with ties of love; I lifted
the yoke from their neck
and bent down to feed them . . . I will
heal their waywardness and love them
freely, for my anger has turned away
from them. I will be like the dew to
Israel; he will blossom like a lily. Like
a cedar of Lebanon he will send down
his roots; his young shoots will grow.
His splendor will be like an olive tree,
his fragrance like a cedar of Lebanon."

Hosea 11:1–4; 14:4–6

GOD'S LOVE IN THE NEW TESTAMENT

Jesus came into the world to show God's love

When Jewish scholars in Alexandria compiled a Greek version of the Hebrew Old Testament, which became known as the Septuagint, the word *agape* came into its own. It is used 95 times out of 100 by the Septuagint translation:

- "Filled with compassion Jesus [touched and healed a man with leprosy]" (Mark 1:41–42).
- "For God so loved the world that he gave his one and only Son, that whoever believes in him shall not perish but have eternal life" (John 3:16).
- "A new commandment I give you: Love one another. As I have loved you, so you must love one another. By this all men will

know that you are my disciples, if you love one another" (John 13:34–35).

- "But God demonstrates his own love for us in this: While we were still sinners, Christ died for us" (Romans 5:8).
- "The life I live in the body, I live by faith in the Son of God, who loved me and gave himself for me" (Galatians 2:20).
- "The fruit of the Spirit is love" (Galatians 5:22).

THE SUPREME EXPRESSION OF GOD'S LOVE: JESUS' DEATH

"Whoever does not love does not know God, because God is love. This is how God showed his love among us: He sent his one and only Son into the world that we might live through him. This is love: not that we loved God, but that he loved us and sent his Son as an atoning sacrifice for our sins. Dear friends, since God so loved us, we also ought to love one another."

᭧ *1 John 4:8–11*

TRANSLATIONS OF PAUL'S HYMN OF LOVE

"Love is patient,
. . . *slow to lose patience (JBP)*
love is kind.
. . . *looks for a way of being constructive (JBP)*
It does not envy,
. . . *love is not jealous (RSV)*
it does not boast,
. . . *not puffed up (KJV)*
it is not proud.
. . . *not arrogant (RSV)*
It is not rude,
. . . *doth not behave itself unseemly (KJV)*
it is not self-seeking,
. . . *does not insist on its own way (RSV)*
it is not easily angered,
. . . *it is not touchy (JBP)*
it keeps no record of wrongs.
not resentful (RSV)
Love does not delight in evil
. . . *does not rejoice at wrong (RSV)*
but rejoices with the truth.
. . . *but is happy with the truth (GNB)*
It always protects,
. . . *love bears all things (RSV)*
always trusts,
. . . *love believes all things (RSV)*
always hopes,
. . . *hopes all things (RSV)*
always perseveres.
. . . *endures all things (RSV)*
And now these three remain: faith, hope and love. But the greatest of these is love."

᭧ *I Corinthians 13:4–7, 13*

Jesus' death on the cross was the supreme expression of God's love for us.

Satan Unmasked

THE NAMES OF SATAN

Satan is the Hebrew word for adversary. Satan is mentioned 36 times in the New Testament. Devil comes from the Greek word *diabolos*, meaning accuser or slanderer. The devil is referred to 33 times in the New Testament.

THE ACTIVITIES OF SATAN

Satan's actions reveal what he does as the enemy of God and God's followers.

- **He stops unbelievers from believing**
  "The god of this age has blinded the minds of unbelievers, so that they cannot see the light of the gospel of the glory of Christ" (2 Corinthians 4:4).

- **He is the Christian's enemy**
  "Your enemy the devil prowls around like a roaring lion looking for someone to devour. Resist him, standing firm in the faith" (1 Peter 5:8–9).

- **He is a liar and father of lies**
  "When he lies, he speaks his native language, for he is a liar and the father of lies" (John 8:44).

- **He leads the whole world astray**
  "The devil, or Satan, . . . leads the whole world astray" (Revelation 12:9).

- **He is a murderer**
  "He was a murderer from the beginning" (John 8:44).

- **He has no truth in him**
  "He [does] not hold to the truth, for there is not truth in him" (John 8:44).

- **He is at work in the hearts of non-Christians**
  "The spirit who is now at work in those who are disobedient" (Ephesians 2:2).

Satan is sometimes described as a serpent or snake.

SATAN'S NAMES		
Name	**Context**	**Reference**
Accuser	The accuser of our brothers.	Revelation 12:10
Ancient serpent	The great dragon was hurled down—that ancient serpent.	Revelation 12:9
Abaddon (Destroyer)	Whose name in Hebrew is Abaddon.	Revelation 9:11
Apollyon (Destroyer)	Whose name . . . in Greek is Apollyon.	Revelation 9:11
Beelzebub	Beelzebub, the prince of the demons.	Matthew 12:24
Belial	What harmony is there between Christ and Belial?	2 Corinthians 6:15
The evil one	The evil one snatches away God's word.	Matthew 13:19
The great dragon	The great dragon was hurled down.	Revelation 12:9
Prince of this world	The prince of this world will be driven out.	John 12:31
Ruler of the kingdom of the air	When you followed the ways of the world and of the ruler of the kingdom of the air.	Ephesians 2:2

JESUS VERSUS SATAN

Jesus Christ is God.
Satan is a created being.
The Son of God appeared . . .
. . . to destroy the devil's work (1 John 3:8).
Jesus was tempted in the desert
. . .by the devil (Matthew 4:1–11).
Jesus showed his superiority
over the devil
when he successfully resisted him.
Through Jesus' death and resurrection . . .
Satan's power over us is shattered.

Christians have the armor of God
to protect them in their battle
against Satan.

HOW TO WIN AGAINST THE DEVIL

- **Resist him**
  "Resist the devil, and he will flee from you"
  (James 4:7).

- **Come close to God**
  "Come near to God and he will come near
  to you" (James 4:18).

- **Clothed in God's armor**
  Christians are engaged in a fierce
  spiritual battle and need the "full
  armor of God" to resist the devil's
  schemes (Ephesians 6:10–17).

- **Prayer**
  Prayer is the Christian's
  resource against Satan and
  demons (Ephesians 6:18).

"And having disarmed the powers and
authorities, [Christ] made a public spectacle of
them, triumphing over them by the cross."

Colossians 2:15.

"So that by his death he
might destroy him who holds the power
of death—that is, the devil—and free those
who all their lives were held in slavery
by their fear of death."

Hebrews 2:14–15

*Prayer is one of
the most effective
weapons.*

THE DEMONS ARE EXPELLED

The demoniac in the synagogue at Capernaum	Mark 1:21–28
The dumb demoniac	Matthew 9:32–34
The daughter of the Canaanite woman	Matthew 15:21–28; Mark 7:24–30
The Gadarene demoniacs	Matthew 8:28–34; Luke 8:26–39
The blind and mute demoniac	Matthew 12:22; Luke 11:14
The epileptic child	Matthew 17:14–21

The End of the World

THE SECOND COMING

The Bible teaches that history is moving to a definite conclusion. This present age will end when Christ comes again.

This event is sometimes called Jesus' second coming, although this is not a phrase found in the Bible.

The last days and the last times
The Old Testament prophets spoke about dramatic events taking place in the "last days." "In the last days" is a phrase frequently used by the prophets (Isaiah 2:2; Micah 4:1). See also Acts 2:16–21 quoting Joel 2:28–32, "In the last days, God says, I will pour out my Spirit on all people" (Acts 2:17).

The New Testament writers make it plain that we live in the last days now.

The last days refer to the time between the first coming of Jesus (advent) and his second coming.

The writer to the Hebrews says, "In these last days [God] has spoken to us by his Son" (Hebrews 1:2).

Peter states, "[Christ] was chosen before the creation of the world, but was revealed in these last times for your sake" (1 Peter 1:20).

The one big future event
The Bible teaches that Jesus will return again.

The end is imminent
The New Testament frequently refers to the coming of Jesus as if it were getting near.

JESUS' SECOND COMING

It will be personal **and** bodily

"This same Jesus, who has been taken from you into heaven, will come back in the same way you have seen him go into heaven" (Acts 1:11).

It will be visible

"So Christ was sacrificed once to take away the sins of many people; and he will appear a second time, not to bear sin, but to bring salvation to those who are waiting for him" (Hebrews 9:28).

"We know that when he appears, we shall be like him, for we shall see him as he is" (1 John 3:2).

It will be sudden

"Therefore keep watch because you do not know when the owner of the house will come back—whether in the evening, or at midnight, or when the cock crows, or at dawn. If he comes suddenly, do not let him find you sleeping" (Mark 13:35–36).

Matthew records these words of Jesus, "I tell you the truth, some who are standing here will not taste death before they see the Son of Man coming in his kingdom" Matthew 16:28).

Peter writes, "The end of all things is near" (1 Peter 4:7).

The date is unknown
The precise date of Jesus' return is not known, so it is fruitless to speculate about this or calculate it, as many have tried to do:

"No one knows about that day or hour, not even the angels in heaven, nor the Son, but only the Father" (Matthew 24:36).

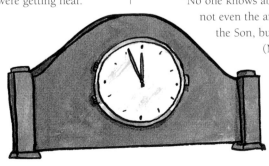

Time is ticking away.

No one knows for certain when the end will come.

SIGNS OF THE TIMES

Before the end comes, certain events must take place: "When you see all these things, you know that it is near, right at the door" (Matthew 24:33). Some perceive in the state of the world in general, and in the formation of the state of Israel in particular, that these events have already taken place, or have nearly all taken place.

- The fall of Jerusalem (Luke 21:5–7).
- False teachers. "The Spirit clearly says that in later times some will abandon the faith and follow deceiving spirits and things taught by demons" (1 Timothy 4:1). See also 2 Timothy 3:1–9; 2 Peter 1–3; 1 John 2:18–19; 4:3.
- Wars. "You will hear of wars and rumors of wars, but see to it that you are not alarmed. Such things must happen, but the end is still to come" (Matthew 24:6).

- Disasters. "There will be famines and earthquakes in various places. All these are the beginning of the birth pains" (Matthew 24:7–8).
- Christians persecuted. "Then you will be handed over to be persecuted and put to death, and you will be hated by all nations because of me" (Matthew 24:9).
- The gospel preached throughout the world (Matthew 24:14).

The antichrist

The New Testament teaches that before the end comes, the antichrist will appear. The antichrist will be able to perform false miracles and will be inspired by Satan. He is sometimes referred to as the lawless one (2 Thessalonians 2:9–10).

The return of Jesus

The return of Jesus will spell the end: "For as lightning that comes from the east is visible even in the west, so will the coming of the Son of Man . . . They will see the Son of Man coming on the clouds of the sky, with power and great glory" (Matthew 24:27, 30).

Earthquakes and volcanic eruptions may signal the end of the world.

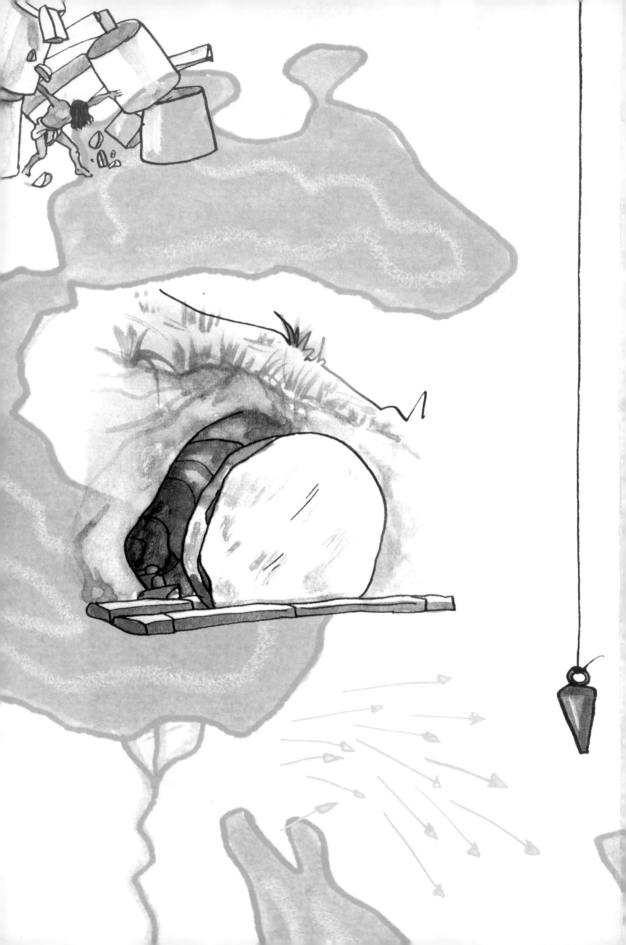

Bible Summary

106–107
How is the Bible Inspired?

108–109
Old Testament Chronology

110–111
Setting of the Old Testament Books

112–113
Pentateuch: Five Books of the Law

114–115
Historical Books of the Old Testament

116–117
Hebrew Poetry

118–119
Prophetic Books of the Old Testament (1)

120–121
Prophetic Books of the Old Testament (2)

122–123
New Testament Chronology

124–125
Setting of the New Testament Books

126–127
The Gospels' Teaching about Jesus

How is the Bible Inspired?

INSPIRED BY GOD

"All Scripture is God-breathed and is useful for teaching, rebuking, correcting, and training in righteousness, so that the man of God may be thoroughly equipped for every good work" (2 Timothy 3:16).

Some translations begin this verse, "All Scripture is inspired by God." In Greek "inspired by God" (*theopneustos*) literally means "God-breathed."

This does not mean that God breathed into the writers, or that God breathed into their writings to make them special. "God-breathed" means that what the writers wrote was breathed out by God. The New Testament writers were God's spokesmen.

Revelation

The Bible is a revelation about God. God is beyond our finite understanding: "Can you fathom the mysteries of God? Can you probe the limits of the Almighty?" (Job 11:7). God revealed, literally "unveiled," himself when he made himself known through the pages of Scripture.

THE WORD OF GOD

In the Bible, the Word of God is likened to:

A lamp	Psalm 119:105
A light	Psalm 119:105
Water	Ephesians 5:26
Seed	1 Peter 1:23
Fire	Jeremiah 20:8–9
Sword	Hebrews 4:12
Hammer	Jeremiah 23:29
Spiritual food	Jeremiah 15:16
Honey	Psalm 119:103
Bread	Matthew 4:4
Milk	I Peter 2:2
Meat	Hebrews 5:12–14

God used a variety of ways to communicate with the Bible writers.

It is *God's* word

Again and again the Old Testament writers took pains to point out that what they were communicating was God's word.

The prophets continually say, "thus says the LORD" or "the word of the LORD came to me" (Exodus 34:27; 1 Chronicles 28:19; Jeremiah 36:1–2).

Verbal inspiration?

God's revelation of himself was through the words the writers of the Bible used: "This is what we speak, not in words taught us by human wisdom but in words taught by the Spirit, expressing spiritual truths in spiritual words" (1 Corinthians 2:13).

GOD SPOKE THROUGH MEN

In one sense, the Bible has two authors: God and the human Bible writers. God did not use the Bible writers like a personal computer performing a purely mechanical task. Their character was not obliterated in what they wrote, and God communicated with them in a variety of ways:

- visions
- voices
- dreams
- world events
- angels
- directly to them. "The Spirit of the LORD spoke through me; his word was on my tongue" (2 Samuel 23:2).

WHAT DID GOD WANT TO ACHIEVE THROUGH THE SCRIPTURES?

To make Jesus' testimony known

"These are the Scriptures that testify about me" (John 5:39).

To make us holy, separate, sanctified, set apart

"Sanctify them by the truth; your word is truth" (John 17:17).

To give us spiritual life

"He chose to give us birth through the word of truth" (James 1:18).

To produce faith

"Faith comes from hearing the message, and the message is heard through the word of Christ" (Romans 10:17).

To search our hearts

"For the word of God is living and active. Sharper than any double-edged sword, it penetrates even to dividing soul and spirit, joint and marrow; it judges the thoughts and attitudes of the heart" (Hebrews 4:12).

To make us wise

"The statutes of the Lord are trustworthy, making wise the simple" (Psalm 19:7).

To give victory over Satan

"Put on the full armor of God so that you can take your stand against the devil's schemes . . . Take the helmet of salvation and the sword of the Spirit, which is the word of God" (Ephesians 6:11, 17).

To give us examples to follow and warnings to heed

"These things happened to them as examples and were written down as warnings to us" (Corinthians 10:11).

To make us wise concerning salvation

"From infancy you have known the holy scriptures, which are able to make you wise for salvation through faith in Christ Jesus" (2 Timothy 3:15).

The Bible is a revelation about God, who is beyond our finite understanding.

But this did not cancel out the personality of the writers of the Bible.

In this sense, the Bible is both the word of men and the word of God. Both of these descriptions are true. The prophet Isaiah could say, "For the mouth of the LORD has spoken" (Isaiah 1:20); and the writer to the Hebrews could write, "In the past God spoke to our forefathers through the prophets at many times and in various ways" (Hebrews 1:1).

Christians believe in the *plenary* inspiration of the Bible. This teaches that what the Bible writers said on all the topics they touched on came from God. It also means that God prompted them so that each truth should be expressed in a particular way. So Scripture is God's Word, and it states exactly what God planned to say.

The Bible is both the word of men and the word of God.

Old Testament Chronology

TIME LINE OF THE OLD TESTAMENT

Dates
A number of the dates in the time line are only approximate. All dates are B.C., before Christ.

Books of the Bible
These are placed in the chart according to the period of history to which they relate, rather than in the order in which they were written. It is not possible to place certain books accurately.

Date	Event	Old Testament book
Before 2000	Creation, Fall, Flood, Babel	Genesis 1–11
2000–1700	The Ancestors of the Israelites, the Patriarchs	Genesis 12–50
2166	Birth of Abram	
2091	Abraham moves to Canaan	
2080	Birth of Ishmael	
2066	Birth of Isaac	
2050	Abraham offers Isaac as a sacrifice	
2006	Birth of Jacob and Esau	
1991	Death of Abraham	
1929	Jacob flees to Haran	
1915	Joseph is born	
1898	Joseph is sold into Egypt	
1859	Death of Jacob	
1805	Death of Joseph	
1700–1250	The Israelites in Egypt: Slavery and Liberation	Exodus
1527	Birth of Moses	Leviticus
1446	The Exodus and crossing the Red Sea	Numbers
1445	The law given at Mount Sinai: the Ten Commandments	Deuteronomy
1406	Death of Moses	
1375	Death of Joshua	Joshua
1250–1030	Conquest and Settlement of Canaan	Ruth
1375–1050	The judges	Judges
1105	Birth of Samuel	
1095–1075	Samson's exploits against the Philistines	
1040	Birth of David	

TIME LINE OF THE OLD TESTAMENT

Date	Event	Old Testament Book
1030–931	The Single Kingdom of Israel	1 Samuel 10–1 Kings 11
1003	David is crowned King of all Israel	Proverbs
970	Death of David, Solomon becomes king	Song of Solomon
966–959	Temple is built	Ecclesiastes
931–722	The Divided Kingdom	1 Kings 12–2 Kings 17
875–848	Elijah	Obadiah, Joel, Jonah, Amos,
848–797	Elisha	Micah, Hosea
722	Fall of the northern kingdom of Samaria to Assyria	Isaiah
722–586	The End of the Kingdom of Judah	Nahum, Habakkuk, Zephaniah
586	Fall of Jerusalem and Judah to Babylon. Temple destroyed.	Jeremiah, Ezekiel
586–400	The Exile and the Return from Exile	Daniel, Haggai
586	Jews are exiled from Jerusalem to Babylon	Zechariah, Esther
538	Jews return to Jerusalem under Zerubbabel	Ezra, Nehemiah, Malachi
457	Second return of Jews with Ezra	
445	Third return of Jews under Nehemiah, who becomes governor	
400–6 B.C.	Between the Old Testament and the New Testament	
	This period of history is not covered by the Bible.	

See also: *New Testament Chronology*, pp. 122–123.

The Setting of the Old Testament Books

To "place" the Old Testament books in our minds, it is helpful to see what parts of the Middle East they refer to.

For example, a map helps us to realize the extent of Jonah's disobedience to God, as he set off to Tarshish, which was in the complete opposite direction to Nineveh, (Jonah 1:1–3).

These maps show some of the places where people in the Bible lived.

BOOKS OF THE OLD TESTAMENT

The 39 books of the Old Testament, which are all about Jewish history and religion, can be divided as follows:

The Pentateuch
• Genesis
• Exodus
• Leviticus
• Numbers
• Deuteronomy

The historical books
• Joshua
• Judges
• Ruth
• 1 Samuel
• 2 Samuel
• 1 Kings
• 2 Kings
• 1 Chronicles
• 2 Chronicles
• Ezra
• Nehemiah
• Esther

The poetical books
• Job
• Psalms
• Proverbs
• Ecclesiastes
• Song of Solomon

The major prophets
• Isaiah
• Jeremiah
• Lamentations
• Ezckiel
• Daniel

The minor prophets
• Hosea
• Joel
• Amos
• Obadiah
• Jonah
• Micah
• Nahum
• Habakkuk
• Zephaniah
• Haggai
• Zechariah
• Malachi

THE PURPOSE OF THE OLD TESTAMENT

Its purpose is to reveal the person and work of the coming Redeemer. The risen Jesus explained to the two people walking to Emmaus that the Old Testament scriptures were all about him. "Beginning with Moses and all the Prophets, [Jesus] explained to them what was said in all the Scriptures concerning himself" (Luke 24:27).

See also: *The Old Testament Books of the Law*, pp. 112–113; *The History Books of the Old Testament*, pp. 114–115; *Hebrew Poetry*, pp. 116–117; *The Prophetic Books of the Old Testament* (1), pp. 118–119; *The Prophetic Books of the Old Testament* (2), pp. 120–121.

The Middle East

1 Ararat mountain range – Noah's ark comes to rest here.
2 Ur – God calls Abraham to follow him from Ur.
3 Egypt – Joseph rises to become prime minister.
4 River Nile – Moses is hidden as a baby in bulrushes.
5 Egypt – The ten plagues
6 Egypt – Moses leads God's people out of Egypt.
7 The wilderness – The Israelites feed on quail in their wilderness wanderings.
8 Sinai – The Ten Commandments are given to Moses.
9 Phoenicia (see map of Canaan) – King Solomon imports cedarwood for building the Temple.
10 Damascus – General Naaman lived here.
11 Babylon – The Jews were exiled here.
12 Nineveh – Jonah preached here.
13 Babylon – One of the exiles in Babylon, Daniel, survives being thrown to the lions.
14 Jerusalem – Under Ezra and Nehemiah the Jews return and rebuild the temple and the city walls.

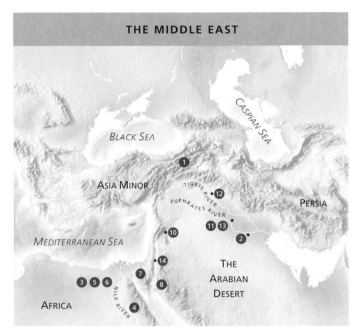

THE MIDDLE EAST

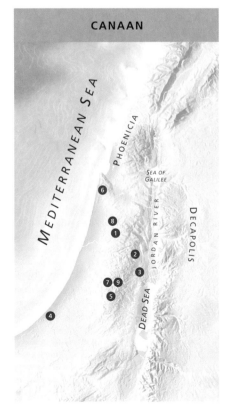

CANAAN

Canaan Map

1 Mount Moriah – A ram saves Isaac from being sacrificed by Abraham.
2 Bethel – Jacob dreams about a stairway between earth and heaven.
3 Jericho – The walls of Jericho fall as Joshua invades Canaan.
4 Gaza – Samson brings down the temple to Dagon and is killed.
5 Bethlehem – David was born in Bethlehem.
6 Mount Carmel – Elijah confronts the prophets of Baal.
7 Jerusalem – David makes Jerusalem his capital city. The prophets Isaiah and Jeremiah preach to the people of Jerusalem.
8 Samaria – The capital city of Israel is destroyed by the Assyrians in 722 BC.
9 Jerusalem – The capital city of Judah is destroyed by the Babylonians in 587 BC.

Pentateuch: Five Books of the Law

Genesis

The name Genesis comes from a Greek word meaning "origin, source, generation or beginning." The original title in Hebrew is Bereshith, which means "in the beginning."

Exodus

Exodus—the book

Greek title: Exodus. Exodus means "departure," "exit," and "going out."

Hebrew title: We'elleh Shemoth, meaning "And these are the names," from the first phrase of Exodus 1:1.

Exodus—the word

The word exodus embodies the main theme of the book: redemption.

The word exodus is used twice in the New Testament. On the first occasion, it is directly linked with Jesus and his redemption.

In Luke 9:31, the word is used in the middle of the description of Jesus' transfiguration: "[Moses and Elijah] spoke about [Jesus'] departure [literally, exodus], which he was about to bring to fulfillment at Jerusalem."

In 2 Peter 1:15, Peter is talking about his own death: "And I will make every effort to see that after my departure [literally exodus] you will always be able to remember these things."

Leviticus

The Greek translators used the name Leviticus for this book, because it deals with the Levitical priesthood. Leviticus was the handbook that was used by the priests of Israel.

Chapters 1–17 are concerned with sacrifice, and chapters 18–27 are about sanctification

Numbers

Other names given to this book are "the book of journeys" and "the book of murmurings."

The pivotal verses in Numbers are Numbers 14:22–23: "Not one of the men who saw my glory and the miraculous signs I performed in Egypt and in the desert but who disobeyed me and tested me ten times —not one of them will ever see the land I promised on oath to their forefathers."

Deuteronomy

Hebrew title: Haddebharim, meaning "the words," taken from the opening phrase of the book, "These are the words."

The English title Deuteronomy comes from the Greek title Deuteronomion, meaning "second law."

This book records the parting words of the aged godly leader to the new generation who will enter the promised land. Before he died, Moses was taken by God to a high mountain from where he was able to view the promised land (Deuteronomy 34: 1–4).

ELEVEN UNITS OF GENESIS	
Introduction to the generations	1:1–2:3
Heaven and earth	2:4–4:26
Adam	5:1–6:8
Noah	6:9–9:29
Sons of Noah	10:1–11:9
Shem	11:10–26
Terah	11:27–25:11
Ishmael	25:12–18
Isaac	25:19–35:29
Esau	36:1–37:1
Jacob	37:2–50:26

THE BOOKS OF THE LAW

The first five books of the Old Testament—Genesis, Exodus, Leviticus, Numbers, Deuteronomy—are known as the Pentateuch (literally: the five-volumed book or five scrolls).

In the Old Testament the Pentateuch is referred to as:

the law (Ezra 10:3)

the Book of the Law of Moses (Nehemiah 8:1)

the Book of Moses (Nehemiah 13:1)

the Law of the Lord (1 Chronicles 16:40)

the Law of God (Nehemiah 10:28)

the Book of the Law of God (Nehemiah 8:18)

the Book of the Law of the Lord (Nehemiah 9:3)

the Law of Moses (Daniel 9:11)

In the New Testament the Pentateuch is referred to as:

the Book of the Law (Galatians 3:10)

the Book of Moses (Mark 12:26)

the Law of the Lord (Luke 2:23–24)

Deuteronomy and "remember"

The book of Deuteronomy sets out ten things which should not be forgotten:

- The giving of the law (4:9–10)
- The Lord's covenant (4:23)
- Slavery in Egypt (5:15)
- God's judgment on Egypt (7:18)
- God's provision (8:2–6)
- Israel's rebellion against God (9:7)
- Deliverance from Egypt (16:3)
- God's punishment (24:9)
- The power of their enemies (25:17).
- The days of old (32:7).

The Israelites are instructed that they should never forget what God has done for them: "Remember that you were slaves in Egypt and that the Lord your God brought you out of there with a mighty hand and an oustretched arm" (Deuteronomy 5:15).

God created food for the Israelites when they were most in need of it.

See also: *Setting of Old Testament Books*, pp. 110–111; *Historical Books of the Old Testament*, pp. 114–115; *Hebrew Poetry*, pp. 116–117; *Prophetic Books of the Old Testament* (1), pp. 118–119; *Prophetic Books of the Old Testament* (2), pp. 120–121.

KEYS TO THE PENTATEUCH

Book	Key chapter	Key verse	Key word	Key people/events
Genesis	12	1:2	Descendants	Abraham, Isaac, Jacob, Joseph
Exodus	12	6:6	Redemption	Exodus, Passover, Tabernacle
Leviticus	16	20:7–8	Holiness	Priesthood, Day of Atonement
Numbers	14	14:22 3	Wanderings	Wandering in the wilderness
Deuteronomy	27	10:12–3	Remember	Moses' three sermons

Historical Books of the Old Testament

THE HISTORICAL BOOKS

The twelve historical books pick up the story of Israel where it left off at the close of the book of Deuteronomy. These books trace the history of the Israelites from their entry into Canaan, the overthrow of the two kingdoms of Israel and Judah, and the Israelites' time of captivity in foreign lands until they eventually return home.

The historical books of the Old Testament can be divided into three groups:

- The theocratic books
- The monarchical books
- The restoration books.

Theocratic books

The theocratic books— Joshua, Judges, and Ruth—focus on the conquest of Canaan and settling down in that country during the time of the Judges. They record the period of Israel's history before they had kings, when they were supposed to have God as their King.

Key verses of the theocratic books

- Joshua 11:23: "So Joshua took the entire land, just as the LORD had directed Moses, and he gave it as an inheritance to Israel according to their tribal divisions."
- Judges 21:25: "In those days Israel had no king; everyone did as he saw fit."
- Ruth 1:16: "But Ruth replied, 'Don't urge me to leave you or to turn back from you. Where you go I will go, and where you stay I will stay. Your people will be my people and your God my God.'"

Monarchical books

The six monarchical books—1 and 2 Samuel, 1 and 2 Kings, and 1 and 2 Chronicles— record the history of Israel's monarchy. It began in 1043 B.C. and ended in 586 B.C.

"To obey is better than sacrifice, and to heed is better than the fat of rams."

KEYS TO THE HISTORY BOOKS				
Book	**Key chapter**	**Key verse**	**Key word**	**Key people/events**
Joshua	1	11:23	Conquest	Possession of the Promised Land
Judges	2	21:25	Delivered	Deborah, Barak, Gideon, Samson
Ruth	4	1:16	Kinsman-redeemer	Naomi, Ruth, Boaz
1 Samuel	8	15:22	King or kingdom	Samuel, last judge; Saul, first king
2 Samuel	11	5:12	King	David's triumphs and troubles
1 Kings	12	11:11	Division	Solomon, Rehoboam, Elijah, Ahab
2 Kings	2	23:27	Evil	Captivity of Israel and Judah
1 Chronicles	1	29:11	Reigned	Genealogical tables, David's reign
2 Chronicles	7	7:14	Established	Solomon, Rehoboam, Judah's kings
Ezra	6	7:10	Build	Return under Zerubbabel and Ezra
Nehemiah	1	6:15	Walls	Rebuilding the walls of Jerusalem
Esther	8	4:14	Deliverance	Esther, Haman, Mordecai. Feast of Purim

*The restoration books describe
the return of some of the Jews
to Jerusalem.*

Key verses of the monarchical books

- 1 Samuel 15:22: "But Samuel replied: 'Does the LORD delight in burnt offerings and sacrifices as much as in obeying the voice of the LORD? To obey is better than sacrifice, and to heed is better than the fat of rams.'"
- 2 Samuel 5:12: "And David knew that the LORD had established him as king over Israel and had exalted his kingdom for the sake of his people Israel.'"
- 1 Kings 11:11: "So the LORD said to Solomon, 'Since this is your attitude and you have not kept my covenant and my decrees, which I commanded you, I will most certainly tear the kingdom away from you and give it to one of your subordinates.'"
- 2 Kings 23:27: "So the LORD said, 'I will remove Judah also from my presence as I removed Israel, and I will reject Jerusalem, the city I chose, and this temple, about which I said, "There shall my Name be."' "
- 1 Chronicles 29:11: "Yours, O LORD, is the greatness and the power and the glory and the majesty and the splendor, for everything in heaven and earth is yours. Yours, O LORD, is the kingdom; you are exalted as head over all."
- 2 Chronicles 7:14: "If my people, who are called by my name, will humble themselves and pray and seek my face and turn from their wicked ways, then will I hear from heaven and will forgive their sins and will heal their land."

Restoration books

The restoration books—Ezra, Nehemiah, and Esther—include the story of the return of a minority of Jews to their homeland after 70 years of captivity. Zerubbabel, Ezra, and Nehemiah were their three leaders.

Key verses of the restoration books

- Ezra 7:10: "For Ezra had devoted himself to the study and observance of the Law of the LORD, and to teaching its decrees and laws in Israel."
- Nehemiah 6:15: "So the wall was completed on the twenty-fifth of Elul, in fifty-two days."
- Esther 4:14: "For if you remain silent at this time, relief and deliverance for the Jews will arise from another place, but you and your father's family will perish. And who knows but that you have come to royal position for such a time as this?"

*The Jews returned to
their homeland after
70 years in captivity.*

See also: *Setting of Old Testament Books,* pp. 110–111; *Old Testament Books of the Law,* pp. 112–113; *Hebrew Poetry,* pp. 116–117; *Prophetic Books of the Old Testament* (1), pp. 118–119; *Prophetic Books of the Old Testament* (2), pp. 120–121.

Hebrew Poetry

The Old Testament has five books classified as poetical books:

- Job
- Psalms
- Proverbs
- Ecclesiastes
- Song of Solomon.

Three types of poetry

The five Old Testament poetry books include three types of poetry.

- Didactic poetry—teaching about life from maxims (Proverbs and Ecclesiastes).
- Lyric poetry—originally accompanied by a lyre (most of the Psalms).
- Dramatic poetry—dialogue in poetic form (Job and Song of Solomon).

The book of Lamentations is one long poem, a dirge lamenting the fall and destruction of the city of Jerusalem. More Hebrew poetry is found, for example, in Judges and Isaiah.

CHARACTERISTICS OF HEBREW POETRY

Parallelism

Hebrew poetry is not based on rhyming words. Instead it is based on rhyming ideas—called parallelism.

One kind of parallelism is Emblematic Parallelism, which provides a visible symbol for something that is abstract. In the example below, the second line is explained by a symbol used in the first line.

> As the deer pants for streams of water,
> so my soul pants for you, O God.
>
> *☙ Psalm 42:1*

Vivid figures of speech

Many of the figures of speech used in Hebrew poetry are also used in other kinds of poetry we are familiar with.

It may seem strange at first sight to say, as Psalm 63:7 does, that we sing in the shadow of God's wings. Taken literally, this would make God a bird! But this is just a figure of speech, a zoomorphism, which is common in Hebrew poetry.

The following seven figures of speech are found in the Hebrew poetry of the Bible.

Perhaps the most famous metaphor in the Bible is "The Lord is my Shepherd."

> "Do you not know? Have you not heard?
> The Lord is an everlasting God, the
> Creator of the ends of the earth. He will
> not grow tired or weary, and his
> understanding no one can fathom. He
> gives strength to the weary and
> increases the power of the weak. Even
> youths grow tired and weary, and
> young men stumble and fall; but those
> who hope in the Lord will renew their
> strength. They will soar on wings like
> eagles; they will run and not grow
> weary, they will walk and not be faint."
>
> *☙ Isaiah 40:28–31*

Metaphor

A comparison in which one thing is said to be another.

Perhaps the most famous one is "The LORD is my Shepherd" (Psalm 23:1).

Simile

Two similar things that are compared to each other.

God's care for his followers is compared to a shield in Psalm 5:12: "For surely, O LORD, you bless the righteous; you surround them with your favour as with a shield."

Hyperbole

An exaggeration to make a point.

Psalm 6:6 is a good example of this: "I am worn out with groaning; all night long I flood my bed with weeping and drench my couch with tears."

Rhetorical question

A question used to confirm or deny a fact.

The Psalmist isn't actually questioning what God is like when he asks in Psalm 35:10, "Who is like you, O LORD?" Rather, he is using a rhetorical question to highlight how wonderful God is in rescuing the poor and needy.

The implication is that no one is like God in doing this.

Personification

Giving a lifeless object human characteristics.

A dramatic example of personification comes in Psalm 77:16: "The waters saw you, O God, the waters saw you and writhed; the very depths were convulsed."

"The waters saw you, O God, the waters saw you and writhed; the very depths were convulsed."

Anthropomorphism

Assigning part of the human body to God in order to teach some truth about God.

When the psalmist refers to God's ears, he is not suggesting that God actually has physical human ears. Rather he is anthropomorphising God in Psalm 31:2 when he asks God to listen to him, using the words, "Turn your ears to me."

Zoomorphism

A word meaning assigning part of the body of an animal to God in order to teach some truth about God.

Psalm 91:4, where God's "feathers" and "wings" are pictured, is a good example of this, because it conjures up such a wonderful image of God caring for us: "He will cover you with his feathers and under his wings you will find refuge."

See also: *Setting of the Old Testament Books*, pp. 110–111; *Old Testament Books of the Law*, pp. 112–113; *Historical Books of the Old Testament*, pp. 114–115; *Prophetic Books of the Old Testament (1)*, pp. 118–119; *Prophetic Books of the Old Testament (2)*, pp. 120–121.

Prophetic Books of the Old Testament (1)

The major and minor prophets left written records of their teachings.

THREE TYPES OF PROPHETS

Major and minor prophets

The major prophets refers to the longer prophetic books of Isaiah, Jeremiah, Ezekiel and Daniel, and the shorter book of Lamentations. The minor prophets refers to the shorter prophetic books.

The oral prophets

The major and minor prophets left written records of their teachings. There are also a number of prophets in the Old Testament, who left no written records that have survived. Such prophets are called the oral prophets.

The minor prophets

The twelve minor prophets, from Obadiah to Malachi, cover a period of 400 years when three different world empires ruled: Assyria, Babylonia, and Persia.

Very little is known about the background of most of these individual prophets.

FOUR THEMES

Both the minor and the major prophets had four basic prophetic themes running through their books.

- The prophets exposed the sinful actions of the people.
- The prophets called the people back to follow God's laws.
- The prophets warned the people about God's impending judgment.
- The prophets anticipated the coming of the Messiah.

The oral prophets like Elijah left no written account of their prophecies.

THE BIBLE PROPHETS		
Major prophets	**Minor prophets**	**Oral prophets**
Isaiah	Hosea	Nathan
Jeremiah	Joel	Ahijah
Lamentations	Amos	Iddo
Ezekiel	Obadiah	Jehu
Daniel	Jonah	Elijah
	Micah	Elisha
	Nahum	Oded
	Habakkuk	Shemaiah
	Zephaniah	Azariah
	Haggai	Hanani
	Zechariah	Jahaziel
	Malachi	Huldah

THEMATIC SURVEY OF THE OLD TESTAMENT PROPHETIC BOOKS

Book	Key chapter	Key verse	Key word	Key theme
Isaiah	53	9:6–7	Salvation	Salvation from God for Israel and the nations
Jeremiah	31	2:19	Return	Turn from apostasy and idolatry back to God
Lamentations	3	3:22–23	Tears	God's sorrow and love for his people Israel
Ezekiel	37	37:14	Visions	The glory of the Lord
Daniel	2	2:44	Kingdom	The adventures of Daniel and his three friends
Hosea	3	4:6	Return	The love of God
Joel	2	2:13	Repent	The day of the Lord
Amos	9	7:8	Plumb line	God's judgment on Israel
Obadiah	1	verse 15	Edom	God's judgment on Edom
Jonah	2	3:2	Preach	Salvation extends to the Gentiles
Micah	7	6:8	Hear	The sin of Israel and the love of God
Nahum	3	1:7–8	Jealous	The destruction of Nineveh
Habakkuk	3	2:4	Faith	The just shall live by faith
Zephaniah	3	2:8	Seek	The day of the Lord
Haggai	2	1:8	Build	Rebuilding the temple
Zechariah	14	1:3	Return	God's love and care for his people
Malachi	4	4:2	Elijah	God's appeal to backsliders

Prophets warned about God's judgment and the return of the Messiah.

See also: *Setting of the Old Testament Books*, pp. 110–111; *Old Testament Books of the Law*, pp. 112–113; *Historical Books of the Old Testament*, pp. 114–115; *Prophetic Books of the Old Testament (2)*, pp. 120–121.

WHO THE MINOR PROPHETS PROPHESIED TO

The Northern Kingdom of Israel	The Southern Kingdom of Judah	Post-exile Jews returned to Jerusalem
Jonah	Obadiah	Haggai
Amos	Joel	Zechariah
Hosea	Micah	Malachi
	Nahum	
	Zephaniah	
	Habakkuk	

Prophetic Books of the Old Testament (2)

THE PROPHETIC BOOKS

The purpose of the prophets was to shed light, God's light, on dark places. "And we have the word of the prophets made more certain, and you will do well to pay attention to it, as to a light shining in a dark place, until the day dawns and the morning star rises in your hearts" (2 Peter 1:19).

Biblical prophecy was speaking out the revealed Word of God, whether the message concerned the past, the present, or the future.

THE PROPHETS AND THE CAPTIVITY

The history of God's people, as recorded in the Old Testament, ends with the return of the "remnant" (the rest of the Jews) from their captivity in Babylonia:

- Twelve prophetic books refer to the time before the captivity.
- Two prophetic books refer to the time during the captivity.
- Three prophetic books refer to the time after the captivity.

Key verses of prophetic books before the captivity

- Isaiah 9:6: "For to us a child is born, to us a son is given, and the government will be on his shoulders. And he will be called Wonderful Counsellor, Mighty God, Everlasting Father, Prince of Peace."
- Jeremiah 2:19: "Your wickedness will punish you; your backsliding will rebuke you. Consider then and realize how evil and bitter it is for you when you forsake the LORD your God and have no awe of me."
- Lamentations: 3:22–23: "Because of the LORD's great love we are not consumed, for his compassions never fail. They are new every morning; great is your faithfulness."

"Look, I am setting a plumb line among my people Israel."

- Hosea 4:6: "My people are destroyed from lack of knowledge."
- Joel 2:13: "Rend your heart and not your garments. Return to the LORD your God, for he is gracious and compassionate, slow to anger and abounding in love, and he relents from sending calamity."
- Amos 7:8: "And the LORD asked me, 'What do you see, Amos?' 'A plumb line,' I replied. Then the Lord said, 'Look, I am setting a plumb line among my people Israel; I will spare them no longer.'"
- Obadiah 15: "The day of the LORD is near for all nations. As you have done, it will be done to you; your deeds will return upon your own head."
- Jonah 3:2: "Go to the great city of Nineveh and proclaim to it the message I give you."

"Go to the great city of Nineveh and proclaim to it the message I give you."

left to another people. It will crush all those kingdoms and bring them to an end, but it will itself endure for ever."

Key verses of prophetic books after the captivity

- Haggai 1:8: "Go up into the mountains and bring down timber and build the house, so that I may take pleasure in it and be honored."
- Zechariah 1:3: "Return to me,' declares the LORD Almighty, 'and I will return to you.'"
- Malachi 4:2: "But for you who revere my name, the sun of righteousness will rise with healing in its wings."

"I will put my Spirit in you and you will live, and I will settle you in your own land. Then you will know that I the LORD have spoken, and I have done it, declares the LORD."

- Micah 6:8: "What does the LORD require of you? To act justly and to love mercy and to walk humbly with your God."
- Nahum 1:7–8: "The LORD is good, a refuge in times of trouble. He cares for those who trust in him, but with an overwhelming flood he will make an end of Nineveh; he will pursue his foes into darkness."
- Habakkuk 2:4: "The righteous will live by his faith."
- Zephaniah 2:3: "Seek the LORD, all you humble of the land, you who do what he commands. Seek righteousness, seek humility; perhaps you will be sheltered on the day of the LORD's anger."

Key verses of prophetic books during the captivity

- Ezekiel 37:14: "I will put my Spirit in you and you will live, and I will settle you in your own land. Then you will know that I the LORD have spoken, and I have done it, declares the LORD."
- Daniel 2:44: "In the times of those kings, the God of heaven will set up a kingdom that will never be destroyed, nor will it be

See also: *Setting of the Old Testament Books*, pp. 110–111; *Old Testament Books of the Law*, pp. 112–113; Historical *Books of the Old Testament*, pp. 114–115; *Hebrew Poetry*, pp. 116–117; *Prophetic Books of the Old Testament (1)*, pp. 118–119.

New Testament Chronology

NEW TESTAMENT CHRONOLOGY

Dates

The date of the birth of Jesus is now often taken as around 4 to 6 B.C., since the calculations for the transition from B.C. to A.D. were found to have been inaccurate.

• A number of the dates in the chart are only approximate.

• A.D. stands for Anno Domini, "in the year of our Lord."

Books of the Bible

These are placed in the chart according to the period of history to which they relate, rather than in the order in which they were written.

Date	New Testament events	New Testament book	Roman emperors/event
4 B.C.–A.D. 30	**The Life of Jesus**	Matthew	Augustus 30 B.C.–A.D. 14
4 B.C.	Birth of Jesus	Mark	Tiberius A.D. 14–37
A.D. 8	Jesus in the temple, age 12	Luke	
A.D. 26	John the Baptist starts his public ministry	John	
	Jesus starts his public ministry		
A.D. 26–36			Pontius Pilate, Roman procurator
A.D. 27–28	John the Baptist imprisoned		
A.D. 29	John the Baptist beheaded		
	Jesus at the Feast of Tabernacles		
A.D. 30	Jesus is crucified and rises again		
	Jesus' ascension		
	The Holy Spirit comes at Pentecost		
A.D. 30–A.D. 100	**The Early Church**	**The Acts of the Apostles**	
A.D. 37	Saul of Tarsus is converted (Paul)		Caligula A.D. 37–41
A.D. 44	James (John's brother) is martyred	James	Claudius A.D. 41–54
A.D. 47–49	Paul's first missionary journey		
A.D. 50	The counsel meets at Jerusalem	Galatians	

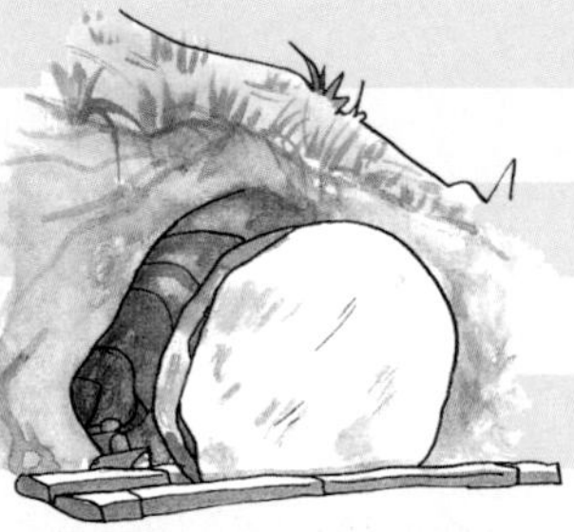

The entrance stone was found rolled away from Jesus' tomb on the third day.

NEW TESTAMENT CHRONOLOGY

Date	New Testament events	New Testament book	Roman emperors/event
A.D. 51–53	Paul's second missionary journey	1 & 2 Thessalonians	
A.D. 54–57	Paul's third missionary journey	Romans, 1 & 2 Corinthians	Nero A.D. 54–68
A.D. 58	Paul arrested in Jerusalem		
A.D. 60	Paul appeals to Caesar		
A.D. 61–2	Paul's two-year house arrest in Rome	Ephesians, Colossians	
? A.D. 62	James (the Lord's brother) is martyred	Philemon, Philippians	
A.D. 64			Nero burns Rome
A.D. 66	Paul's second imprisonment in Rome	1 & 2 Peter, 1 & 2 Timothy, Titus, Jude	
? A.D. 67–8	Peter and Paul martyred in Rome		Galba, Otho, Vitelius, A.D. 69
			Vespasian A.D. 69–79
			Titus A.D. 79–81
A.D. 70	Jerusalem falls. The temple is destroyed	Hebrews	
A.D. 81–96	Christians persecuted by Domitian		
A.D. 90–5	Apostle John exiled on Patmos	1,2 & 3 John, Revelation	Nerva A.D. 96–98

John was exiled on an Aegean island where he wrote Revelation.

See also: *Old Testament Chronology*, pp. 108–109.

The Setting of the New Testament Books

BOOKS OF THE NEW TESTAMENT

The 27 New Testament books are divided into the following categories:
- Gospels
- History
- The Letters of Paul
- Letters not written by Paul
- Apocalyptic writings

THE SEAS

Both the early and the later ministries of Jesus, and the journeys of Paul, were closely connected with the sea.

Many of Jesus' miracles took place on or near the sea. Twice he increased the fishing catch of his disciples (Luke 5:4–11; John 21:1–11), he calmed a storm (Matthew 8:23–27), and walked on the water (Mark 6:48–51). The Sermon on the Mount took place at Capernaum which was near the Sea of Galilee.

The Mediterranean Sea was a crucial means of journeying from place to place for the apostles spreading the word of Christ after he had died. Many of the towns where Paul preached were on the coast, and John was exiled on the island of Patmos in the Aegean, where he wrote Revelation.

THE BOOKS OF THE NEW TESTAMENT

Gospels	History	The Letters of Paul
Matthew	Acts	Romans
Mark		1 Corinthians
Luke		2 Corinthians
John		Galatians
		Ephesians

The Letters of Paul	Letters not written by Paul	Apocalyptic writing
Philippians	Hebrews	Revelation
Colossians	James	
1 Thessalonians	1 Peter	
2 Thessalonians	2 Peter	
1 Timothy	1 John	
2 Timothy	2 John	
Titus	3 John	
Philemon	Jude	

Map of the Mediterranean Sea

This map plots the route of Paul's journey to Rome. Many of the towns Paul wrote his letters to are still thriving, but others are now in ruins.
- **Rome:** Paul wrote Romans to the Christians of Rome, where he had dozens of Christian friends. Peter's two letters, 1 and 2 Peter, were probably written from Rome
- **Corinth:** Paul wrote a number of letters to Corinth, but we only have two left, 1 and 2 Corinthians.
- **Galatia:** Paul wrote his most severe letter, Galatians, to the church of Galatia.
- **Ephesus:** Paul's letter to the Ephesians, may have been intended for a wide area surrounding Ephesus, and not just the Christians in the town itself. John's three letters, 1, 2, and 3 John were written from Ephesus.
- **Philippi:** Paul's letter to the Philippians indicates that this was one of his "favorite" churches.
- **Colossae:** Paul's letter to the Colossians ranks as one of the most Christ-centered books of the Bible. Philemon lived in Colossae and received a short personal letter from Paul, asking him to take back his runaway slave Onesimus, who had met up with Paul in Rome. We know this letter as Philemon.
- **Thessalonica:** Paul wrote two letters to the Christians at Thessalonica, 1 and 2 Thessalonians.
- **Macedonia:** Paul wrote his letters 1 and 2 Timothy to his young friend and pastor, Timothy, while in Macedonia.
- **Crete:** While ministering to the Christians on the island of Crete Titus received a letter from Paul, which we now call Titus.
- **Jerusalem:** The letter we now know as James was probably written from Jerusalem.
- **Patmos:** The island where John wrote the book of Revelation

Bible scholars are not sure where Jude's short letter, Jude, or the writer of Hebrews were written from.

The Sea of Galilee

In this area Jesus' early ministry, as recorded by the four gospel writers, took place.
- **Cana:** Jesus changed water into wine at a wedding held there, John 2:1–11. On his second visit there, Jesus cured the nobleman's son, John 4:46–54.

PAUL'S ROUTE FROM JERUSALEM TO ROME

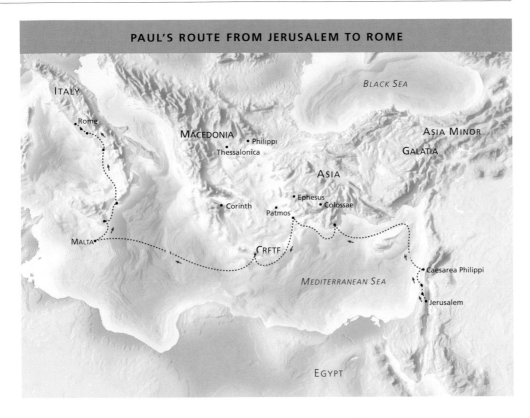

- **Nazareth:** Jesus was brought up here as a boy. He was later rejected and almost killed by its people, Luke 4:16–30.
- **Capernaum:** Jesus gave the Sermon on the Mount close to Capernaum, Matthew 5–8.
- **Nain:** Jesus raised to life the son of the widow of Nain, Luke 7:11–16.
- **Gadara:** Jesus healed the demoniac in this area, Mark 5:1–20.
- **Bethsaida:** Jesus performed the miracle of feeding 5000 people with five loaves and two fish near here, Mark 6:30–44.
- **Gennesaret:** After Jesus had walked on the water of the Sea of Galilee, they landed at Gennesaret, Mark 6:45–56.

Map of the Sea of Galilee and the Dead Sea

This map shows Jesus' later ministry, as recorded by Matthew, Mark, Luke and John.
- **Machaerus:** John the Baptist was beheaded here, Mark 6:14–29.
- **Tyre:** Jesus ministered in the region of Tyre and Sidon, Mark 7:24–30.
- **Decapolis:** Jesus healed a deaf-mute in this region, Mark 7:31–37.
- **Caesarea Philippi:** Peter says, "You are the Christ" here, Mark 8:27:30.
- **Samaria:** Jesus is rejected by the Samaritans here, Luke 9:51–56.
- **Ephraim:** Jesus withdrew from the public to the quiet of this village, John 11:54–57.
- **Jerusalem:** Jesus entered in triumph at the start of his last week, Mark 11:1–11.

THE SEA OF GALILEE AND THE DEAD SEA

The Gospels' Teaching about Jesus

JESUS ON JESUS

There is no better way to learn about who Jesus was, what he said and did, and why he lived than to study what Jesus had to say about himself.

JESUS AS LION IN MATTHEW'S GOSPEL: "JESUS IS KING"

The first verse of Matthew announces the arrival of the Anointed One:
"A record of the genealogy of Jesus Christ the son of David" (Matthew 1:1).

The presentation of the King: 1:1–4:11. As David's direct descendant, Jesus is qualified to be Israel's King.

The proclamation of the King: 4:12–7:29. These words are especially found in the Sermon on the Mount, 5–7.

The power of the King: 8:1–11:1. Ten miracles, 8–9, support the claims of Jesus.

The gradual rejection of the King: 11:2–16:12.

The preparation of the King's disciples: 16:13–20:28. Jesus shows the importance of accepting his offer of righteousness.

The presentation and rejection of the King: 20:29–27:66. Most of this section is aimed at those who reject Jesus as King. "Are you the king of the Jews?" "Yes . . ." (27:11).

The proof of the King: 28. The resurrection authenticates the words of the King.

JESUS IN THE GOSPELS

Each gospel depicts Jesus in a rather different way:
- Matthew depicts Jesus as King.
- Mark depicts Jesus as Servant.
- Luke depicts Jesus as Man.
- John depicts Jesus as God.

Symbols for the Gospels
Four symbols are found in Ezekiel's vision: "Their faces looked like this: Each of the four had the face of a man, and on the right side each had the face of a lion, and on the left the face of an ox; each also had the face of an eagle" (Ezekiel 1:10).

The same four symbols are found in a vision in the book of Revelation: "The first living creature was like a lion, the second was like an ox, the third had a face like a man, the fourth was like a flying eagle" (Revelation 4:7).

Commentators of the four gospels have applied the following four symbols to the four gospels:

WHERE JESUS TEACHES ABOUT HIMSELF		
Gospel	**Chapter and verse**	
Matthew	16:13–21	20:17–19
	26:26–35	
Mark	8:31–38	10:32–34
Luke	4:16–30	9:21–27
	9:43–45	18:31–34
	20:1–8	24:13–49
John	2:13–22	3:1–21
	5:19–47	6:25–71
	7:16–31	7:37–38
	8:12–59	9:3–5
	9:35–41	10:1–42
	11:17–27	12:27–36
	14–17	